# THE YALE SHAKESPEARE

EDITED BY

WILBUR L. CROSS     TUCKER BROOKE
WILLARD HIGLEY DURHAM

PUBLISHED UNDER THE DIRECTION
OF THE
DEPARTMENT OF ENGLISH, YALE UNIVERSITY
ON THE FUND
GIVEN TO THE YALE UNIVERSITY PRESS IN 1917
BY THE MEMBERS OF THE
KINGSLEY TRUST ASSOCIATION
TO COMMEMORATE THE SEVENTY-FIFTH ANNIVERSARY
OF THE FOUNDING OF THE SOCIETY

·: *The Yale Shakespeare* :·

# THE LIFE AND DEATH
# OF KING JOHN

EDITED BY

**STANLEY T. WILLIAMS**

**NEW HAVEN AND LONDON**

**YALE UNIVERSITY PRESS**

# TABLE OF CONTENTS

*The facsimile opposite represents, from a copy in the Yale Elizabethan Club, the title-page of the third edition of the old play of the 'Troublesome Reign of John' upon which 'King John' was based. This edition, which appeared the year before the first edition of Shakespeare's play in the Folio of 1623, bears the false statement that it was 'Written by W. Shakespeare.' See Appendix A, p. 117.*

# THE

## First and second Part of

the troublesome Raigne of
IOHN King of England.

*With the discouerie of King* Richard Cor-
delions Base sonne (vulgarly named, the Bastard
*Fauconbridge:* ) Also the death of King
*Iohn* at Swinstead Abbey.

*As they were ( sundry times ) lately acted.*

---

Written by W. SHAKESPEARE.

---

LONDON,
Printed by *Aug: Mathewes* for *Thomas Dewe,* and are to
be sold at his shop in St. Dunstones Churchyard in Fleet-street, 1622, ƒ

# [DRAMATIS PERSONÆ.

King John

Prince Henry, *Son to the King*

Arthur, *Duke of Britaine, Nephew to the King*

The Earl of Pembroke

The Earl of Essex

The Earl of Salisbury

The Lord Bigot

Hubert de Burgh

Robert Faulconbridge, *Son to Sir Robert Faulconbridge*

Philip the Bastard, *his half-brother*

James Gurney, *Servant to Lady Faulconbridge*

Peter of Pomfret, *a Prophet*

Philip, *King of France*

Lewis, *the Dauphin*

Lymoges, *Duke of Austria*

Cardinal Pandulph, *the Pope's Legate*

Melun, *a French Lord*

Chatillion, *Ambassador from France*

Queen Elinor, *Mother to King John*

Constance, *Mother to Arthur*

Blanch of Spain, *Niece to King John*

Lady Faulconbridge

Lords, Ladies, Citizens of Angiers, Sheriff, Heralds, Officers, Soldiers, Executioners, Messengers, and other Attendants.

Scene: *Sometimes in England, and sometimes in France.*]

# The Life and Death of King John

## ACT FIRST

### Scene One

*[London. A Room of State in the Palace]*

*Enter King John, Queen Elinor, Pembroke, Essex, and Salisbury, [and Others,] with the Chatillion of France.*

  *K. John.* Now, say, Chatillion, what would France
    with us?

  *Chat.* Thus, after greeting, speaks the King of
    France,
In my behaviour, to the majesty,
The borrow'd majesty, of England here.        **4**

  *Eli.* A strange beginning: 'borrow'd majesty'!

  *K. John.* Silence, good mother; hear the embassy.

  *Chat.* Philip of France, in right and true behalf
Of thy deceased brother Geoffrey's son,        **8**
Arthur Plantagenet, lays most lawful claim
To this fair island and the territories,
To Ireland, Poitiers, Anjou, Touraine, Maine;
Desiring thee to lay aside the sword        **12**
Which sways usurpingly these several titles,
And put the same into young Arthur's hand,
Thy nephew and right royal sovereign.

  *K. John.* What follows if we disallow of this?    **16**

  *Chat.* The proud control of fierce and bloody war,

---

The Life and Death of King John; *cf. n.*
Scene One. S.d. the Chatillion of France; *cf. n*
3 In my behaviour: *as represented in my person and outward acts*
6 embassy: *ambassador's commission or message*
7 in . . . behalf: *for the benefit of*      10 this fair island; *cf. n.*
13 *Cf. n.*                  16 disallow of: *refuse*

To enforce these rights so forcibly withheld.

    *K. John.* Here have we war for war, and blood for
    blood,

Controlment for controlment: so answer France.    20

    *Chat.* Then take my king's defiance from my mouth,
The farthest limit of my embassy.

    *K. John.* Bear mine to him, and so depart in peace:
Be thou as lightning in the eyes of France;    24
For ere thou canst report I will be there,
The thunder of my cannon shall be heard.
So, hence! Be thou the trumpet of our wrath,
And sullen presage of your own decay.    28
An honourable conduct let him have:
Pembroke, look to 't.    Farewell, Chatillion.

                *Exit Chat[illion] and Pem[broke].*

    *Eli.* What now, my son! have I not ever said
How that ambitious Constance would not cease    32
Till she had kindled France and all the world
Upon the right and party of her son?
This might have been prevented and made whole
With very easy arguments of love,    36
Which now the manage of two kingdoms must
With fearful bloody issue arbitrate.

    *K. John.* Our strong possession, and our right, for
    us.

    *Eli.* Your strong possession much more than your
    right,    40
Or else it must go wrong with you and me:
So much my conscience whispers in your ear,
Which none but heaven, and you, and I, shall hear.

---

20 Controlment: *restraint*            26 cannon; *cf. n.*
28 sullen: *gloomy*    decay: *ruin*       29 conduct: *escort*
34 Upon: *in defense of*    party: *cause*
35 made whole: *restored to health*
36 easy: *slight*    arguments: *discussions*    37 manage: *management*

*Enter a Sheriff [who whispers to Essex].*

*Essex.* My liege, here is the strangest contro-
versy,                                                                    44
Come from the country to be judg'd by you,
That e'er I heard: shall I produce the men?

*K. John.* Let them approach.
Our abbeys and our priories shall pay                    48
This expedition's charge.

*Enter Robert Faulconbridge, and Philip [his bastard
brother].*

                                    What men are you?
*Bast.* Your faithful subject, I, a gentleman,
Born in Northamptonshire, and eldest son,
As I suppose, to Robert Faulconbridge,                  52
A soldier, by the honour-giving hand
Of Cordelion knighted in the field.

*K. John.* What art thou?

*Rob.* The son and heir to that same Faulcon-
bridge.                                                                   56

*K. John.* Is that the elder, and art thou the heir?
You came not of one mother then, it seems.

*Bast.* Most certain of one mother, mighty king,
That is well known; and, as I think, one father.    60
But for the certain knowledge of that truth
I put you o'er to heaven and to my mother:
Of that I doubt, as all men's children may.

*Eli.* Out on thee, rude man! thou dost shame thy
mother                                                                   64
And wound her honour with this diffidence.

*Bast.* I, madam? no, I have no reason for it;
That is my brother's plea and none of mine;

48, 49 Our abbeys . . . charge; *cf. n.*        49 expedition's; *cf. n*
54 Cordelion; *cf. n.*    62 put . . . o'er: *refer*    65 diffidence: *distrust*

The which if he can prove, a' pops me out                    68
At least from fair five hundred pound a year:
Heaven guard my mother's honour and my land!

   *K. John.* A good blunt fellow.  Why, being younger
     born,
Doth he lay claim to thine inheritance?                      72

   *Bast.* I know not why, except to get the land.
But once he slander'd me with bastardy:
But whe'r I be as true-begot or no,
That still I lay upon my mother's head;                      76
But that I am as well-begot, my liege,—
Fair fall the bones that took the pains for me!—
Compare our faces and be judge yourself.
If old Sir Robert did beget us both,                         80
And were our father, and this son like him;
O old Sir Robert, father, on my knee
I give heaven thanks I was not like to thee!

   *K. John.* Why, what a madcap hath heaven lent us
     here!                                                     84

   *Eli.* He hath a trick of Cordelion's face;
The accent of his tongue affecteth him.
Do you not read some tokens of my son
In the large composition of this man?                        88

   *K. John.* Mine eye hath well examined his parts,
And finds them perfect Richard. Sirrah, speak:
What doth move you to claim your brother's land?

   *Bast.* Because he hath a half-face, like my father. 92
With half that face would he have all my land;
A half-fac'd groat five hundred pound a year!

   *Rob.* My gracious liege, when that my father liv'd,
Your brother did employ my father much,—     96

   *Bast.* Well, sir, by this you cannot get my land:

68 a': *he*   74 once: *once for all*   75 whe'r: *whether*   78 fall: *befall*
85 trick: *peculiar or characteristic expression*        86 affecteth: *imitates*
88 composition: *constitution*                           92 half-face: *thin face*
94 A half-fac'd groat; *cf. n.*

Your tale must be how he employ'd my mother.
  *Rob.* And once dispatch'd him in an embassy
To Germany, there with the emperor              100
To treat of high affairs touching that time.
Th' advantage of his absence took the king,
And in the mean time sojourn'd at my father's;
Where how he did prevail I shame to speak,          104
But truth is truth: large lengths of seas and shores
Between my father and my mother lay,—
As I have heard my father speak himself,—
When this same lusty gentleman was got.           108
Upon his death-bed he by will bequeath'd
His lands to me, and took it on his death
That this my mother's son was none of his;
And if he were, he came into the world            112
Full fourteen weeks before the course of time.
Then, good my liege, let me have what is mine,
My father's land, as was my father's will.
  *K. John.* Sirrah, your brother is legitimate;     116
Your father's wife did after wedlock bear him,
And if she did play false, the fault was hers;
Which fault lies on the hazards of all husbands
That marry wives. Tell me, how if my brother,    120
Who, as you say, took pains to get this son,
Had of your father claim'd this son for his?
In sooth, good friend, your father might have kept
This calf bred from his cow from all the world;     124
In sooth he might; then, if he were my brother's,
My brother might not claim him; nor your father,
Being none of his, refuse him: this concludes;
My mother's son did get your father's heir;        128
Your father's heir must have your father's land.

---

104 shame: *am ashamed*      108 lusty: *merry*      got: *begotten*
110 took it on his death: *gave a strong assurance*
119 lies on the hazards: *is among the chances*
127 refuse: *disown*      concludes: *settles the matter*

*Rob.* Shall then my father's will be of no force
To dispossess that child which is not his?

   *Bast.* Of no more force to dispossess me, sir,   132
Than was his will to get me, as I think.

   *Eli.* Whether hadst thou rather be a Faulconbridge
And like thy brother, to enjoy thy land,
Or the reputed son of Cordelion,   136
Lord of thy presence and no land beside?

   *Bast.* Madam, and if my brother had my shape,
And I had his, Sir Robert's his, like him;
And if my legs were two such riding-rods,   140
My arms such eel-skins stuff'd, mv face so thin
That in mine ear I durst not stick a rose
Lest men should say, 'Look, where three-farthings
     goes!'
And, to his shape, were heir to all this land,   144
Would I might never stir from off this place,
I would give it every foot to have this face;
I would not be Sir Nob in any case.

   *Eli.* I like thee well: wilt thou forsake thy for-
     tune,   148
Bequeath thy land to him, and follow me?
I am a soldier and now bound to France.

   *Bast.* Brother, take you my land, I'll take my
     chance.
Your face hath got five hundred pound a year,   152
Yet sell your face for five pence and 'tis dear.
Madam, I'll follow you unto the death.

   *Eli.* Nay, I would have you go before me thither.

   *Bast.* Our country manners give our betters way.  156

   *K. John.* What is thy name?

---

134 Whether . . . rather: *wouldst thou rather; cf. n.*
137 presence: *person*
                                        158 and if: *an if, if*
139 Sir Robert's his, like him; *cf. n.*     140 riding-rods: *switches*
142, 143 *Cf. n.*     144 to: *in addition to*     147 Sir Nob; *cf. n.*
149 Bequeath: *bestow*     150 bound: *intending to go*

*Bast.* Philip, my liege, so is my name begun;
Philip, good old Sir Robert's wife's eldest son.

*K. John.* From henceforth bear his name whose
    form thou bearest:  160
Kneel thou down Philip, but rise more great;
Arise Sir Richard, and Plantagenet.

*Bast.* Brother by th' mother's side, give me your
    hand:
My father gave me honour, yours gave land.  164
Now blessed be the hour, by night or day,
When I was got, Sir Robert was away!

*Eli.* The very spirit of Plantagenet!
I am thy grandam, Richard; call me so.  168

*Bast.* Madam, by chance but not by truth; what
    though?
Something about, a little from the right,
    In at the window, or else o'er the hatch:
Who dares not stir by day must walk by night,  172
    And have is have, however men do catch.
Near or far off, well won is still well shot,
And I am I, howe'er I was begot.

*K. John.* Go, Faulconbridge: now hast thou thy
    desire;  176
A landless knight makes thee a landed squire.
Come, madam, and come, Richard, we must speed
For France, for France, for it is more than need.

*Bast.* Brother, adieu; good fortune come to thee!  180
For thou wast got i' th' way of honesty.

                  *Exeunt all but Bastard.*

A foot of honour better than I was;
But many a many foot of land the worse.
Well, now can I make any Joan a lady.  184

---

161 *Cf. n.*    169 truth: *honesty*    what though: *what does it matter?*
170 Something about: *somewhat circuitously*    right: *straight road*
171 hatch: *half-door; cf. n.*    173 *Cf. n.*    177 *Cf. n.*
184 Joan: *peasant girl*

'Good den, Sir Richard!'—'God-a-mercy, fellow!'—
And if his name be George, I'll call him Peter;
For new-made honour doth forget men's names;
'Tis too respective and too sociable                    188
For your conversion. Now your traveller,
He and his toothpick at my worship's mess,
And when my knightly stomach is suffic'd,
Why then I suck my teeth, and catechize               192
My picked man of countries: 'My dear sir,'—
Thus, leaning on mine elbow, I begin,—
'I shall beseech you,'—that is question now;
And then comes answer like an Absey-book:             196
'O, sir,' says answer, 'at your best command;
At your employment; at your service, sir';
'No, sir,' says question, 'I, sweet sir, at yours';
And so, ere answer knows what question would,         200
Saving in dialogue of compliment,
And talking of the Alps and Apennines,
The Pyrenean and the river Po,
It draws toward supper in conclusion so.              204
But this is worshipful society,
And fits the mounting spirit like myself;
For he is but a bastard to the time,
That doth not smack of observation;                   208
And so am I, whether I smack or no;
And not alone in habit and device,
Exterior form, outward accoutrement,
But from the inward motion to deliver                 212
Sweet, sweet, sweet poison for the age's tooth,

185 *Cf. n.*     Good den: *good even*     God-a-mercy: *God reward you*
188 respective: *considerate*
189 For your conversion: *for one who has undergone such a change of
    rank as you have*     189, 190 Now your traveller . . . mess; *cf. n.*
193 picked: *refined*     196 Absey-book: *primer, horn-book*
203 Pyrenean: *Pyrenees*
207 bastard to the time: *no true son of the age*
208 observation: *obsequiousness*
                                                  209-215 *Cf. n.*
210 habit: *dress, bearing*     device: *shape*     212 motion: *impulse*

Which, though I will not practise to deceive,
Yet, to avoid deceit, I mean to learn;
For it shall strew the footsteps of my rising.　　216
But who comes in such haste in riding-robes?
What woman-post is this? hath she no husband
That will take pains to blow a horn before her?

*Enter Lady Faulconbridge and James Gurney.*

O me! 'tis my mother.　How now, good lady!　　220
What brings you here to court so hastily?

　*Lady F.* Where is that slave, thy brother? where
　　is he,
That holds in chase mine honour up and down?

　*Bast.* My brother Robert? old Sir Robert's son?　224
Colbrand the giant, that same mighty man?
Is it Sir Robert's son that you seek so?

　*Lady F.* Sir Robert's son!　Ay, thou unreverend
　　boy,
Sir Robert's son: why scorn'st thou at Sir Robert?　228
He is Sir Robert's son, and so art thou.

　*Bast.* James Gurney, wilt thou give us leave awhile?

　*Gur.* Good leave, good Philip.

　*Bast.*　　　　　　　　Philip! sparrow! James,
There's toys abroad; anon I'll tell thee more.　　232

　　　　　　　　　　　　　　　　*Exit James.*

Madam, I was not old Sir Robert's son:
Sir Robert might have eat his part in me
Upon Good Friday and ne'er broke his fast.
Sir Robert could do well: marry, to confess,　　236
Could he get me?　Sir Robert could not do it.

215 deceit: *being deceived*　　　　　　　216 *Cf. n.*
218 woman-post: *woman-courier*　　　　219 *Cf. n.*
225 Colbrand the giant; *cf. n.*　　　227 unreverend: *irreverent*
228 scorn'st: *mock'st*　　230 give us leave: *permit us to be alone*
231 Philip! sparrow!; *cf. n.*
232 toys: *rumors*　　abroad: *about in the world*　　236 marry: *indeed*
237 *Cf. n.*

We know his handiwork; therefore, good mother,
To whom am I beholding for these limbs?
Sir Robert never holp to make this leg.                    240

*Lady F.* Hast thou conspired with thy brother too,
That for thine own gain shouldst defend mine hon-
 our?
What means this scorn, thou most untoward knave?

 *Bast.* Knight, knight, good mother, Basilisco-
 like.                                                 244
What! I am dubb'd; I have it on my shoulder.
But, mother, I am not Sir Robert's son;
I have disclaim'd Sir Robert and my land;
Legitimation, name, and all is gone.                       248
Then, good my mother, let me know my father;
Some proper man, I hope; who was it, mother?

 *Lady F.* Hast thou denied thyself a Faulconbridge?
 *Bast.* As faithfully as I deny the devil.           252
 *Lady F.* King Richard Cordelion was thy father:
By long and vehement suit I was seduc'd
To make room for him in my husband's bed.
Heaven lay not my transgression to my charge!             256
Thou art the issue of my dear offence,
Which was so strongly urg'd past my defence.

 *Bast.* Now, by this light, were I to get again,
Madam, I would not wish a better father.                   260
Some sins do bear their privilege on earth,
And so doth yours; your fault was not your folly.
Needs must you lay your heart at his dispose,
Subjected tribute to commanding love,                      264
Against whose fury and unmatched force
The aweless lion could not wage the fight,

239 beholding: *indebted*      240 holp: *helped*
243 untoward: *unmannerly* 244 *Cf. n.* 245 dubb'd: *made a knight*
250 proper: *handsome* 257 dear: *grievous* 259 get: *be begotten*
261 *Cf. n.* 263 dispose: *disposal* 264 Subjected: *submissive*
266 aweless: *fearless*

Nor keep his princely heart from Richard's hand.
He that perforce robs lions of their hearts           268
May easily win a woman's.  Ay, my mother,
With all my heart I thank thee for my father!
Who lives and dares but say thou didst not well
When I was got, I'll send his soul to hell.           272
Come, lady, I will show thee to my kin;

   And they shall say, when Richard me begot,
If thou hadst said him nay, it had been sin;

   Who says it was, he lies; I say 'twas not.        276

                           *Exeunt.*


## ACT SECOND

### Scene One

*[France.  Before the Walls of Angiers]*

*Enter before Angiers, Philip, King of France, [and
his Forces,] Lewis [the] Dauphin, Austria [and
his Forces], Constance, Arthur [and Attendants].*

*Lewis.* Before Angiers well met, brave Austria.
Arthur, that great forerunner of thy blood,
Richard, that robb'd the lion of his heart
And fought the holy wars in Palestine,                 4
By this brave duke came early to his grave;
And, for amends to his posterity,
At our importance hither is he come,
To spread his colours, boy, in thy behalf,             8
And to rebuke the usurpation
Of thy unnatural uncle, English John.
Embrace him, love him, give him welcome hither.

267 *Cf. n.*    Act Second; *cf. n.*    Scene One; *cf. n.*    1 Lewis; *cf. n.*
2 forerunner of thy blood; *cf. n.*                                    5 *Cf. n.*
7 importance: *importunity*                                    9 rebuke: *check*

*Arth.* God shall forgive you Cordelion's death    12
The rather that you give his offspring life,
Shadowing their right under your wings of war.
I give you welcome with a powerless hand,
But with a heart full of unstained love.    16
Welcome before the gates of Angiers, duke.

*Lewis.* A noble boy!  Who would not do thee right?

*Aust.* Upon thy cheek lay I this zealous kiss,
As seal to this indenture of my love,    20
That to my home I will no more return
Till Angiers, and the right thou hast in France,
Together with that pale, that white-fac'd shore,
Whose foot spurns back the ocean's roaring tides    24
And coops from other lands her islanders,
Even till that England, hedg'd in with the main,
That water-walled bulwark, still secure
And confident from foreign purposes,    28
Even till that utmost corner of the west
Salute thee for her king: till then, fair boy,
Will I not think of home, but follow arms.

*Const.* O, take his mother's thanks, a widow's
thanks,    32
Till your strong hand shall help to give him strength
To make a more requital to your love.

*Aust.* The peace of heaven is theirs that lift their
swords
In such a just and charitable war.    36

*K. Phi.* Well then, to work our cannon shall be
bent
Against the brows of this resisting town.
Call for our chiefest men of discipline,
To cull the plots of best advantages.    40

14 Shadowing: *sheltering*                    20 indenture: *contract*
25 coops: *encloses for protection or defense*
27 still: *always*          secure: *free from care*          34 more: *greater*
37 bent: *aimed*          39 discipline: *military experience*          40 *Cf. n.*

We'll lay before this town our royal bones,
Wade to the market-place in Frenchmen's blood,
But we will make it subject to this boy.

*Const.* Stay for an answer to your embassy,          44
Lest unadvis'd you stain your swords with blood.
My Lord Chatillion may from England bring
That right in peace which here we urge in war;
And then we shall repent each drop of blood          48
That hot rash haste so indirectly shed.

### Enter Chatillion.

*K. Phi.* A wonder, lady! lo, upon thy wish,
Our messenger, Chatillion, is arriv'd!
What England says, say briefly, gentle lord;          52
We coldly pause for thee; Chatillion, speak.

*Chat.* Then turn your forces from this paltry siege
And stir them up against a mightier task.
England, impatient of your just demands,          56
Hath put himself in arms; the adverse winds,
Whose leisure I have stay'd, have given him time
To land his legions all as soon as I.
His marches are expedient to this town,          60
His forces strong, his soldiers confident.
With him along is come the mother-queen,
An Ate, stirring him to blood and strife;
With her her niece, the Lady Blanch of Spain;          64
With them a bastard of the king's deceas'd;
And all th' unsettled humours of the land,
Rash, inconsiderate, fiery voluntaries,
With ladies' faces and fierce dragons' spleens,          68

---

43 But: *if . . . not*          45 unadvis'd: *inconsiderately*
49 indirectly: *wrongly*          53 coldly: *calmly*          58 stay'd: *waited for*
59 all: *quite*          60 expedient: *expeditious*          63 An Ate; *cf. n.*
64, 65 her niece . . . deceas'd; *cf. n.*
66 unsettled humours: *men of unsettled humor*
67 voluntaries: *volunteers*
68 spleens: *the organ itself viewed as the seat of emotions and passions*

Have sold their fortunes at their native homes,
Bearing their birthrights proudly on their backs,
To make a hazard of new fortunes here.
In brief, a braver choice of dauntless spirits          72
Than now the English bottoms have waft o'er
Did never float upon the swelling tide,
To do offence and scathe in Christendom.
The interruption of their churlish drums              76
Cuts off more circumstance; they are at hand,

                                *Drum beats.*

To parley or to fight; therefore prepare.
    *K. Phi.* How much unlook'd for is this expedition!
    *Aust.* By how much unexpected, by so much          80
We must awake endeavour for defence,
For courage mounteth with occasion.
Let them be welcome then; we are prepar'd.

*Enter K[ing] of England, Bastard, Queen [Elinor],*
       *Blanch, Pembroke, and others.*

    *K. John.* Peace be to France, if France in peace
       permit                                          84
Our just and lineal entrance to our own;
If not, bleed France, and peace ascend to heaven,
Whiles we, God's wrathful agent, do correct
Their proud contempt that beats his peace to
       heaven.                                        88
    *K. Phi.* Peace be to England, if that war return
From France to England, there to live in peace.
England we love; and, for that England's sake
With burden of our armour here we sweat.          92
This toil of ours should be a work of thine;

72 choice: *choice or picked company*
73 bottoms: *ships*    waft: *conveyed by water*    75 scathe: *harm*
77 circumstance: *details*              79 expedition: *speed*
82 occasion: *emergency*    85 lineal: *due by right of descent*
87 Whiles: *while*    correct: *punish*    89 if that: *if*

But thou from loving England art so far,
That thou hast under-wrought his lawful king,
Cut off the sequence of posterity, 96
Outfaced infant state, and done a rape
Upon the maiden virtue of the crown.
Look here upon thy brother Geoffrey's face;
These eyes, these brows, were moulded out of his; 100
This little abstract doth contain that large
Which died in Geoffrey, and the hand of time
Shall draw this brief into as huge a volume.
That Geoffrey was thy elder brother born, 104
And this his son; England was Geoffrey's right
And this is Geoffrey's in the name of God.
How comes it then that thou art call'd a king,
When living blood doth in these temples beat, 108
Which owe the crown that thou o'ermasterest?

 *K. John.* From whom hast thou this great commission, France,
To draw my answer from thy articles?

 *K. Phi.* From that supernal judge, that stirs good
  thoughts 112
In any breast of strong authority,
To look into the blots and stains of right.
That judge hath made me guardian to this boy,
Under whose warrant I impeach thy wrong 116
And by whose help I mean to chastise it.

 *K. John.* Alack! thou dost usurp authority.

 *K. Phi.* Excuse it is to beat usurping down.

 *Eli.* Who is it thou dost call usurper, France? 120

 *Const.* Let me make answer: thy usurping son.

---

95 under-wrought: *undermined*  his: *its*
96 sequence of posterity: *hereditary succession*
97 Outfaced: *intimidated*  infant state: *state that belongs to an infant*  101-103 *Cf. n.*  109 owe: *own*
111 articles: *heads or items in a list or document*
112 supernal: *heavenly*    113, 114 *Cf. n.*
116 impeach: *call in question*  119 Excuse; *cf. n.*

*Eli.* Out, insolent! thy bastard shall be king,
That thou mayst be a queen, and check the world!

   *Const.* My bed was ever to thy son as true    124
As thine was to thy husband, and this boy
Liker in feature to his father Geoffrey
Than thou and John in manners; being as like
As rain to water, or devil to his dam.    128
My boy a bastard! By my soul I think
His father never was so true begot:
It cannot be and if thou wert his mother.

   *Eli.* There's a good mother, boy, that blots thy
    father.    132

   *Const.* There's a good grandam, boy, that would
    blot thee.

   *Aust.* Peace!

   *Bast.*       Hear the crier.

   *Aust.*                What the devil art thou?

   *Bast.* One that will play the devil, sir, with you,
And a' may catch your hide and you alone.    136
You are the hare of whom the proverb goes,
Whose valour plucks dead lions by the beard.
I'll smoke your skin-coat, and I catch you right.
Sirrah, look to 't; i' faith, I will, i' faith.    140

   *Blanch.* O well did he become that lion's robe,
That did disrobe the lion of that robe!

   *Bast.* It lies as sightly on the back of him
As great Alcides' shoes upon an ass.    144
But, ass, I'll take that burthen from your back,
Or lay on that shall make your shoulders crack.

   *Aust.* What cracker is this same that deafs our ears

---

123 That thou mayst be a queen; *cf. n.*      check: *curb*
126 feature: *shape*      127 *Cf. n.*
131 *Cf. n.*    and if: *if*         130 true: *truly*
137 the proverb; *cf. n.*         132 blots: *calumniates*
139 smoke your skin-coat: *give you a drubbing*      right: *properly*
141, 142 *Cf. n.*         141 become: *adorn*
144 Alcides' shoes; *cf. n.*         147 cracker: *boaster*

With this abundance of superfluous breath?          148
King Lewis, determine what we shall do straight.

 *Lewis.* Women and fools, break off your confer-
ence.
King John, this is the very sum of all:
England and Ireland, Anjou, Touraine, Maine,       152
In right of Arthur do I claim of thee.
Wilt thou resign them and lay down thy arms?

 *K. John.* My life as soon!  I do defy thee, France.
Arthur of Britaine, yield thee to my hand;          156
And out of my dear love I'll give thee more
Than e'er the coward hand of France can win.
Submit thee, boy.

 *Eli.*     Come to thy grandam, child.

 *Const.* Do, child, go to it grandam, child;      160
Give grandam kingdom, and it grandam will
Give it a plum, a cherry, and a fig;
There's a good grandam.

 *Arth.*    Good my mother, peace!
I would that I were low laid in my grave;          164
I am not worth this coil that's made for me.

 *Eli.* His mother shames him so, poor boy, he weeps.

 *Const.* Now shame upon you, whe'r she does or no!
His grandam's wrongs, and not his mother's
shames,                                            168
Draws those heaven-moving pearls from his poor eyes,
Which heaven shall take in nature of a fee;
Ay, with these crystal beads heaven shall be brib'd
To do him justice and revenge on you.              172

 *Eli.* Thou monstrous slanderer of heaven and earth!

 *Const.* Thou monstrous injurer of heaven and earth!
Call not me slanderer; thou and thine usurp

---

149 King Lewis; *cf. n.*  straight: *immediately*  150 Lewis; *cf. n.*
156 Britaine; *cf. n.*   157 dear: *heartfelt*   160 it: *its*
165 *Cf. n.*  coil: *disturbance*    169 Draws: *draw*

The dominations, royalties, and rights                    176
Of this oppressed boy.  This is thy eldest son's son,
Infortunate in nothing but in thee:
Thy sins are visited in this poor child;
The canon of the law is laid on him,                       180
Being but the second generation
Removed from thy sin-conceiving womb.

    *K. John.* Bedlam, have done.

    *Const.*                    I have but this to say,
That he is not only plagued for her sin,                   184
But God hath made her sin and her the plague
On this removed issue, plagu'd for her,
And with her plague; her sin his injury;
Her injury the beadle to her sin,                          188
All punish'd in the person of this child,
And all for her, a plague upon her.

    *Eli.* Thou unadvised scold, I can produce
A will that bars the title of thy son.                     192

    *Const.* Ay, who doubts that? a will! a wicked will;
A woman's will; a canker'd grandam's will!

    *K. Phi.* Peace, lady! pause, or be more temperate.
It ill beseems this presence to cry aim                    196
To these ill-tuned repetitions.
Some trumpet summon hither to the walls
These men of Angiers; let us hear them speak
Whose title they admit, Arthur's or John's.                200

    *Trumpet sounds.  Enter a Citizen upon the walls.*

    *Cit.* Who is it that hath warn'd us to the walls?
    *K. Phi.* 'Tis France, for England.
    *K. John.*                              England for itself.

177 eldest; *cf. n.*                              179 visited: *punished*
180 The canon of the law; *cf. n.*    183 Bedlam: *lunatic*    185-190 *Cf. n.*
191 unadvised: *rash*        192 A will; *cf. n.*        194 canker'd: *malignant*
196 cry aim: *give encouragement*                198 trumpet: *trumpeter*
201 warn'd: *summoned*

You men of Angiers, and my loving subjects,—
   *K. Phi.* You loving men of Angiers, Arthur's sub-
     jects,                                                   204
Our trumpet call'd you to this gentle parle,—
   *K. John.* For our advantage; therefore hear us'
     first.
These flags of France, that are advanced here
Before the eye and prospect of your town,                    208
Have hither march'd to your endamagement.
The cannons have their bowels full of wrath,
And ready mounted are they to spit forth
Their iron indignation 'gainst your walls:                   212
All preparation for a bloody siege
And merciless proceeding by these French
Confronts your city's eyes, your winking gates;
And but for our approach those sleeping stones,              216
That as a waist doth girdle you about,
By the compulsion of their ordinance
By this time from their fixed beds of lime
Had been dishabited, and wide havoc made                     220
For bloody power to rush upon your peace.
But on the sight of us your lawful king,
Who painfully with much expedient march
Have brought a countercheck before your gates,              224
To save unscratch'd your city's threaten'd cheeks,
Behold, the French amaz'd vouchsafe a parle;
And now, instead of bullets wrapp'd in fire,
To make a shaking fever in your walls,                       228
They shoot but calm words folded up in smoke,
To make a faithless error in your ears:

205 parle: *parley*             207 advanced: *raised*
208 prospect: *range of vision*    209 endamagement: *injury*
215 Confronts; *cf. n.*    winking: *closed*    217 doth: *do*
218 ordinance: *ordnance, artillery*    220 dishabited: *dislodged*
223 painfully: *laboriously*    expedient: *speedy*
224 countercheck: *check*    226 amaz'd: *dumbfounded*
230 faithless: *disloyal*    error: *confusion*

Which trust accordingly, kind citizens,
And let us in, your king, whose labour'd spirits,     232
Forwearied in this action of swift speed,
Craves harbourage within your city walls.

    *K. Phi.* When I have said, make answer to us both.
Lo! in this right hand, whose protection     236
Is most divinely vow'd upon the right
Of him it holds, stands young Plantagenet,
Son to the elder brother of this man,
And king o'er him and all that he enjoys.     240
For this downtrodden equity, we tread
In warlike march these greens before your town,
Being no further enemy to you
Than the constraint of hospitable zeal,     244
In the relief of this oppressed child,
Religiously provokes.   Be pleased then
To pay that duty which you truly owe
To him that owes it, namely, this young prince;     248
And then our arms, like to a muzzled bear,
Save in aspect, hath all offence seal'd up;
Our cannons' malice vainly shall be spent
Against th' invulnerable clouds of heaven;     252
And with a blessed and unvex'd retire,
With unhack'd swords and helmets all unbruis'd,
We will bear home that lusty blood again
Which here we came to spout against your town,     256
And leave your children, wives, and you, in peace.
But if you fondly pass our proffer'd offer,
'Tis not the rounder of your old-fac'd walls
Can hide you from our messengers of war,     260

232 labour'd: *oppressed with labor*
233 Forwearied: *thoroughly exhausted*          234 harbourage: *shelter*
236 in: *held by*          237 upon: *on the side or party of*     242 greens: *turf*
246 Religiously: *faithfully*          247 owe; *cf. n.*          253 retire: *return*
258 fondly: *foolishly*
259 rounder: *roundure, circuit*          old-fac'd: *venerable*
260 messengers of war: *missiles*

Though all these English and their discipline
Were harbour'd in their rude circumference.
Then tell us, shall your city call us lord,
In that behalf which we have challeng'd it?      264
Or shall we give the signal to our rage
And stalk in blood to our possession?

 *Cit.* In brief, we are the King of England's subjects:
For him, and in his right, we hold this town.      268

 *K. John.* Acknowledge then the king, and let me
  in.

 *Cit.* That can we not; but he that proves the king,
To him will we prove loyal: till that time
Have we ramm'd up our gates against the world.      272

 *K. John.* Doth not the crown of England prove the
  king?
And if not that, I bring you witnesses,
Twice fifteen thousand hearts of England's breed,—

 *Bast.* Bastards, and else.      276

 *K. John.* To verify our title with their lives.

 *K. Phi.* As many and as well-born bloods as those,—

 *Bast.* Some bastards, too.

 *K. Phi.* Stand in his face to contradict his claim.  280

 *Cit.* Till you compound whose right is worthiest,
We for the worthiest hold the right from both.

 *K. John.* Then God forgive the sins of all those
  souls
That to their everlasting residence,      284
Before the dew of evening fall, shall fleet,
In dreadful trial of our kingdom's king!

 *K. Phi.* Amen, Amen! Mount, chevaliers! to arms!

 *Bast.* Saint George, that swing'd the dragon, and
  e'er since      288

276 else: *other kinds*   278 bloods: *men of mettle*   281 compound: *settle*
282 *Cf. n.*      285 fleet: *pass away*      288 swing'd: *thrashed*

Sits on's horseback at mine hostess' door,
Teach us some fence! [*To Austria.*] Sirrah, were I
    at home,
At your den, sirrah, with your lioness,
I would set an ox head to your lion's hide.        292
And make a monster of you.
    *Aust.*                        Peace! no more.
    *Bast.* O! tremble, for you hear the lion roar.
    *K. John.* Up higher to the plain; where we'll set
    forth
In best appointment all our regiments.            296
    *Bast.* Speed then, to take advantage of the field.
    *K. Phi.* It shall be so; [*To Lewis*] and at the other
    hill
Command the rest to stand.  God, and our right!
                                *Exeunt.*

*Here after excursions, Enter the Herald of France
        with Trumpets to the gates.*

    *F. Her.* You men of Angiers, open wide your
    gates,                                        300
And let young Arthur, Duke of Britaine, in,
Who by the hand of France this day hath made
Much work for tears in many an English mother,
Whose sons lie scatter'd on the bleeding ground;  304
Many a widow's husband grovelling lies,
Coldly embracing the discolour'd earth;
And victory, with little loss, doth play
Upon the dancing banners of the French,           308
Who are at hand, triumphantly display'd,
To enter conquerors and to proclaim
Arthur of Britaine England's king and yours.

*Enter English Herald, with trumpet.*

**290** fence: *art of fencing*                    **292** ox head; *cf. n.*

*E. Her.* Rejoice, you men of Angiers, ring your
    bells;        312
King John, your king and England's, doth approach,
Commander of this hot malicious day.
Their armours, that march'd hence so silver-bright,
Hither return all gilt with Frenchmen's blood.    316
There stuck no plume in any English crest
That is removed by a staff of France;
Our colours do return in those same hands
That did display them when we first march'd forth; 320
And, like a jolly troop of huntsmen, come
Our lusty English, all with purpled hands
Dy'd in the dying slaughter of their foes.
Open your gates and give the victors way.    324
  *Cit.* Heralds, from off our towers we might behold,
From first to last, the onset and retire
Of both your armies, whose equality
By our best eyes cannot be censured.    328
Blood hath bought blood, and blows have answer'd
    blows;
Strength match'd with strength, and power confronted
    power.
Both are alike; and both alike we like.
One must prove greatest. While they weigh so
    even,    332
We hold our town for neither, yet for both.

*Enter the two Kings, with their powers, at several
doors.*

  *K. John.* France, hast thou yet more blood to cast
    away?
Say, shall the current of our right run on?
Whose passage, vex'd with thy impediment,    336

314 malicious: *violent*               316 gilt: *reddened*
318 staff: *shaft of a lance*    323 *Cf. n.*    325 *Cit.*; *cf. n.*
326 retire: *retreat*                 328 censured: *estimated*

Shall leave his native channel and o'erswell
With course disturb'd even thy confining shores,
Unless thou let his silver water keep
A peaceful progress to the ocean.                340

    *K. Phi.* England, thou hast not sav'd one drop of
      blood,
In this hot trial, more than we of France;
Rather, lost more.   And by this hand I swear,
That sways the earth this climate overlooks,     344
Before we will lay down our just-borne arms,
We'll put thee down, 'gainst whom these arms we
      bear,
Or add a royal number to the dead,
Gracing the scroll that tells of this war's loss   348
With slaughter coupled to the name of kings.

    *Bast.* Ha, majesty! how high thy glory towers
When the rich blood of kings is set on fire!
O now doth Death line his dead chaps with steel!  352
The swords of soldiers are his teeth, his fangs;
And now he feasts, mousing the flesh of men,
In undetermin'd differences of kings.
Why stand these royal fronts amazed thus?        356
Cry 'havoc!' kings; back to the stained field,
You equal potents, fiery kindled spirits!
Then let confusion of one part confirm
The other's peace; till then, blows, blood, and
      death!                                    360

    *K. John.* Whose party do the townsmen yet admit?

    *K. Phi.* Speak, citizens, for England; who's your
      king?

340 progress: *course*            344 climate: *region of the sky*
345 just-borne: *carried in a just cause*
347 royal number: *a royal item in the list*      350 towers: *soars*
352 *Cf. n.*    line: *strengthen*    chaps: *jaws*
354 mousing: *tearing*               356 fronts: *faces*
357 Cry 'havoc!' kings; *cf. n.*      358 potents: *potentates*
359 confusion: *rout*    part: *party*        361 yet: *now*

   *Cit.* The King of England, when we know the
     king.

   *K. Phi.* Know him in us, that here hold up his
     right.           364

   *K. John.* In us, that are our own great deputy,
And bear possession of our person here,
Lord of our presence, Angiers, and of you.

   *Cit.* A greater power than we denies all this;   368
And, till it be undoubted, we do lock
Our former scruple in our strong-barr'd gates,
Kings of our fear; until our fears, resolv'd,
Be by some certain king purg'd and depos'd.   372

   *Bast.* By heaven, these scroyles of Angiers flout
     you, kings,
And stand securely on their battlements
As in a theatre, whence they gape and point
At your industrious scenes and acts of death.   376
Your royal presences be rul'd by me:
Do like the mutines of Jerusalem,
Be friends awhile and both conjointly bend
Your sharpest deeds of malice on this town.   380
By east and west let France and England mount
Their battering cannon charged to the mouths,
Till their soul-fearing clamours have brawl'd down
The flinty ribs of this contemptuous city.   384
I'd play incessantly upon these jades,
Even till unfenced desolation
Leave them as naked as the vulgar air.
That done, dissever your united strengths,   388
And part your mingled colours once again;

371 Kings of our fear; *cf. n.*         373 scroyles: *scoundrels*
374 securely: *confidently*   376 industrious scenes: *laborious industry*
378 mutines: *mutineers; cf. n.*         379 bend: *direct*
383 soul-fearing: *soul-affrighting*   brawl'd down: *beaten down with
   clamor*        385 jades: *wretches*        386 unfenced: *defenceless*
**387** naked: *unarmed*     vulgar: *common to all*

Turn face to face and bloody point to point;
Then, in a moment, Fortune shall cull forth
Out of one side her happy minion,                            392
To whom in favour she shall give the day,
And kiss him with a glorious victory.
How like you this wild counsel, mighty states?
Smacks it not something of the policy?                       396

    *K. John.* Now, by the sky that hangs above our
       heads,
I like it well.   France, shall we knit our powers
And lay this Angiers even with the ground;
Then after fight who shall be king of it?                    400

    *Bast.* And if thou hast the mettle of a king,
Being wrong'd as we are by this peevish town,
Turn thou the mouth of thy artillery,
As we will ours, against these saucy walls;                 404
And when that we have dash'd them to the ground,
Why then defy each other, and, pell-mell,
Make work upon ourselves, for heaven or hell.

    *K. Phi.* Let it be so.   Say, where will you as-
      sault?                                              408

    *K. John.* We from the west will send destruction
Into this city's bosom.

    *Aust.* I from the north.

    *K. Phi.*                         Our thunder from the south
Shall rain their drift of bullets on this town.             412

    *Bast.* [*Aside.*] O prudent discipline!   From north
      to south
Austria and France shoot in each other's mouth:
I'll stir them to it.   Come, away, away!

---

390 point: *point of the sword*                       392 minion: *darling*
395 states: *persons of rank*
396 something: *somewhat*          policy: *political art*
398 powers: *forces*      400 after: *afterwards*      402 peevish: *obstinate*
404 saucy: *insolent*                              406 pell-mell: *in confusion*
412 drift: *stream*                              413 discipline: *military science*

*Cit.* Hear us, great kings; vouchsafe a while to
　　stay,                                                      416
And I shall show you peace and fair-fac'd league.
Win you this city without stroke or wound;
Rescue those breathing lives to die in beds,
That here come sacrifices for the field.                     420
Persever not, but hear me, mighty kings.

　　*K. John.* Speak on with favour; we are bent to
　　hear.

　　*Cit.* That daughter there of Spain, the Lady
　　Blanch,
Is near to England; look upon the years                      424
Of Lewis the Dauphin and that lovely maid.
If lusty love should go in quest of beauty,
Where should he find it fairer than in Blanch?
If zealous love should go in search of virtue,              428
Where should he find it purer than in Blanch?
If love ambitious sought a match of birth,
Whose veins bound richer blood than Lady Blanch?
Such as she is, in beauty, virtue, birth,                    432
Is the young Dauphin every way complete.
If not complete of, say he is not she;
And she again wants nothing, to name want,
If want it be not that she is not he.                        436
He is the half part of a blessed man,
Left to be finished by such as she;
And she a fair divided excellence,
Whose fulness of perfection lies in him.                     440
O! two such silver currents, when they join,
Do glorify the banks that bound them in;
And two such shores to two such streams made one,
Two such controlling bounds shall you be, kings,             444

421 Persever: *persevere*　　422 favour: *permission*　　bent: *inclined*
425 Dauphin; *cf. n.*　　428 zealous: *öious*　　431 bound: *enclose*
434 complete of: *filled with these qualities*

To these two princes, if you marry them.
This union shall do more than battery can
To our fast-closed gates; for at this match,
With swifter spleen than powder can enforce,        **448**
The mouth of passage shall we fling wide ope,
And give you entrance; but without this match,
The sea enraged is not half so deaf,
Lions more confident, mountains and rocks           **452**
More free from motion, no, not death himself
In mortal fury half so peremptory,
As we to keep this city.

    *Bast.*          Here's a stay,
That shakes the rotten carcase of old Death         **456**
Out of his rags! Here's a large mouth, indeed,
That spits forth death and mountains, rocks and seas,
Talks as familiarly of roaring lions
As maids of thirteen do of puppy-dogs.              **460**
What cannoneer begot this lusty blood?
He speaks plain cannon fire, and smoke and bounce;
He gives the bastinado with his tongue;
Our ears are cudgell'd; not a word of his           **464**
But buffets better than a fist of France.
'Zounds! I was never so bethump'd with words
Since I first call'd my brother's father dad.

    *Eli.* [*Aside to King John.*] Son, list to this conjunc-
    tion, make this match;                        **468**
Give with our niece a dowry large enough;
For by this knot thou shalt so surely tie
Thy now unsur'd assurance to the crown,
That yon green boy shall have no sun to ripe        **472**
The bloom that promiseth a mighty fruit.

---

447 match; *cf. n.*        448 spleen: *energy*      enforce: *compel*
449 ope: *open*    454 peremptory: *resolved*    455 stay: *hindrance*
462 bounce: *bang*           463 bastinado: *beating with a stick*
466 'Zounds: *God's wounds*    468 list: *listen*    471 unsur'd: *insecure*

I see a yielding in the looks of France;
Mark how they whisper: urge them while their souls
Are capable of this ambition,                                476
Lest zeal, now melted by the windy breath
Of soft petitions, pity and remorse,
Cool and congeal again to what it was.

   *Cit.* Why answer not the double majesties        480
This friendly treaty of our threaten'd town?

   *K. Phi.* Speak England first, that hath been forward
     first
To speak unto this city: what say you?

   *K. John.* If that the Dauphin there, thy princely
     son,                                                484
Can in this book of beauty read 'I love,'
Her dowry shall weigh equal with a queen.
For Anjou and fair Touraine, Maine, Poitiers,
And all that we upon this side the sea,                       488
Except this city now by us besieg'd,
Find liable to our crown and dignity,
Shall gild her bridal bed and make her rich
In titles, honours, and promotions,                          492
As she in beauty, education, blood,
Holds hand with any princess of the world.

   *K. Phi.* What sayst thou, boy? look in the lady's
     face.

   *Lew.* I do, my lord; and in her eye I find            496
A wonder, or a wondrous miracle,
The shadow of myself form'd in her eye;
Which, being but the shadow of your son,
Becomes a sun, and makes your son a shadow.                  500
I do protest I never lov'd myself
Till now infixed I beheld myself,

---

476 capable of: *apt to be affected by*       477-479 *Cf. n.*
478 remorse: *compassion*    481 treaty: *proposal tending to agreement*
490 liable: *subject*        494 Holds hand with: *matches*

Drawn in the flattering table of her eye.

                                *Whispers with Blanch.*

*Bast.* Drawn in the flattering table of her eye!    504

Hang'd in the frowning wrinkle of her brow!

And quarter'd in her heart! he doth espy

    Himself love's traitor; this is pity now,

That hang'd and drawn and quarter'd, there should
    be                                      508

In such a love so vile a lout as he.

    *Blanch.* My uncle's will in this respect is mine:

If he see aught in you that makes him like,

That anything he sees, which moves his liking,    512

I can with ease translate it to my will;

Or if you will, to speak more properly,

I will enforce it easily to my love.

Further I will not flatter you, my lord,    516

That all I see in you is worthy love,

Than this: that nothing do I see in you,

Though churlish thoughts themselves should be your
    judge,

That I can find should merit any hate.    520

    *K. John.* What say these young ones? What say
    you, my niece?

    *Blanch.* That she is bound in honour still to do

What you in wisdom still vouchsafe to say.

    *K. John.* Speak then, Prince Dauphin; can you love
    this lady?    524

    *Lew.* Nay, ask me if I can refrain from love;

For I do love her most unfeignedly.

    *K. John.* Then do I give Volquessen, Touraine,
    Maine,

Poitiers, and Anjou, these five provinces,    528

503 table: *board or flat surface on which a picture is painted*
509 so vile a lout; *cf. n.*    511 like: *feel affection*    513 *Cf. n.*
514 properly: *strictly*    519 churlish: *sparing of praise*    527, 528 *Cf. n.*

With her to thee; and this addition more,
Full thirty thousand marks of English coin.
Philip of France, if thou be pleas'd withal,
Command thy son and daughter to join hands.    532

   *K. Phi.* It likes us well.   Young princes, close
     your hands.

   *Aust.* And your lips too; for I am well assur'd
That I did so when I was first assur'd.

   *K. Phi.* Now, citizens of Angiers, ope your gates, 536
Let in that amity which you have made;
For at Saint Mary's chapel presently
The rites of marriage shall be solemniz'd.
Is not the Lady Constance in this troop?    540
I know she is not, for this match made up
Her presence would have interrupted much.
Where is she and her son? tell me, who knows.

   *Lew.* She is sad and passionate at your highness'
     tent.    544

   *K. Phi.* And, by my faith, this league that we have
     made
Will give her sadness very little cure.
Brother of England, how may we content
This widow lady?   In her right we came;    548
Which we, God knows, have turn'd another way,
To our own vantage.

   *K. John.*       We will heal up all;
For we'll create young Arthur Duke of Britaine
And Earl of Richmond; and this rich fair town    552
We make him lord of.   Call the Lady Constance;
Some speedy messenger bid her repair
To our solemnity: I trust we shall,

531 withal: *with this*   533 likes: *pleases*   535 assur'd: *betrothed*
537 that amity: *those friends*   538 presently: *immediately*
541 made up: *which has been arranged*
544 passionate: *full of angry passion*
555 solemnity: *marriage ceremony*

If not fill up the measure of her will,                              556
Yet in some measure satisfy her so,
That we shall stop her exclamation.
Go we, as well as haste will suffer us,
To this unlook'd for, unprepared pomp.                         560

      *Exeunt [all but the Bastard]*. [*The Citizens*
              *retire from the walls.*]

    *Bast.* Mad world! mad kings! mad composition!
John, to stop Arthur's title in the whole,
Hath willingly departed with a part,
And France, whose armour conscience buckled on, 564
Whom zeal and charity brought to the field
As God's own soldier, rounded in the ear
With that same purpose-changer, that sly devil,
That broker, that still breaks the pate of faith,    568
That daily break-vow, he that wins of all,
Of kings, of beggars, old men, young men, maids,
Who, having no external thing to lose
But the word 'maid,' cheats the poor maid of that, 572
That smooth-fac'd gentleman, tickling Commodity,
Commodity, the bias of the world;
The world, who of itself is peized well,
Made to run even upon even ground,                             576
Till this advantage, this vile-drawing bias,
This sway of motion, this Commodity,
Makes it take head from all indifferency,
From all direction, purpose, course, intent.                   580
And this same bias, this Commodity,
This bawd, this broker, this all-changing word,

558 exclamation: *loud complaint*     561 composition: *agreement*
563 departed: *parted*   566 rounded: *whispered*   567 With: *by*
568 broker: *go-between*        569 break-vow: *breaker of promises*
571-574 Cf. n.     573 tickling Commodity: *flattering self-interest*
575 peized: *poised*       577 vile-drawing: *drawing into evil*
578 sway: *direction*
579 take head: *take power,*      from all indifferency: *out of all*
     *moderation*

Clapp'd on the outward eye of fickle France,
Hath drawn him from his own determin'd aid,    584
From a resolv'd and honourable war,
To a most base and vile-concluded peace.
And why rail I on this Commodity?
But for because he hath not woo'd me yet.    588
Not that I have the power to clutch my hand
When his fair angels would salute my palm;
But for my hand, as unattempted yet,
Like a poor beggar, raileth on the rich.    592
Well, whiles I am a beggar, I will rail
And say there is no sin but to be rich;
And being rich, my virtue then shall be
To say there is no vice but beggary.    596
Since kings break faith upon Commodity,
Gain, be my lord, for I will worship thee!    *Exit.*


## ACT THIRD

### Scene One

*[Angiers. The French King's Pavilion]*

*Enter Constance, Arthur, and Salisbury.*

*Const.* Gone to be married! gone to swear a peace!
False blood to false blood join'd! gone to be friends!
Shall Lewis have Blanch, and Blanch those provinces?
It is not so; thou hast misspoke, misheard;    4
Be well advis'd, tell o'er thy tale again;
It cannot be; thou dost but say 'tis so.
I trust I may not trust thee, for thy word
Is but the vain breath of a common man;    8

583 Clapp'd on the outward eye; *cf. n.*    585 resolv'd: *determined upon*
588 But for because: *merely because*       590 fair angels; *cf. n.*
591 for: *because*    unattempted: *untempted*
597 upon: *in consequence of*

Believe me, I do not believe thee, man;
I have a king's oath to the contrary.
Thou shalt be punish'd for thus frighting me,
For I am sick and capable of fears;                           12
Oppress'd with wrongs, and therefore full of fears;
A widow, husbandless, subject to fears;
A woman, naturally born to fears;
And though thou now confess thou didst but jest,   16
With my vex'd spirits I cannot take a truce,
But they will quake and tremble all this day.
What dost thou mean by shaking of thy head?
Why dost thou look so sadly on my son?             20
What means that hand upon that breast of thine?
Why holds thine eye that lamentable rheum,
Like a proud river peering o'er his bounds?
Be these sad signs confirmers of thy words?        24
Then speak again; not all thy former tale,
But this one word, whether thy tale be true.

   *Sal.* As true as I believe you think them false
That give you cause to prove my saying true.       28

   *Const.* O if thou teach me to believe this sorrow,
Teach thou this sorrow how to make me die!
And let belief and life encounter so
As doth the fury of two desperate men              32
Which in the very meeting fall and die.
Lewis marry Blanch! O boy! then where art thou?
France friend with England, what becomes of me?
Fellow, be gone! I cannot brook thy sight:         36
This news hath made thee a most ugly man.

   *Sal.* What other harm have I, good lady, done,
But spoke the harm that is by others done?

   *Const.* Which harm within itself so heinous is  40
As it makes harmful all that speak of it.

---

17 spirits: *feelings*       take a truce: *make peace*
22 lamentable rheum: *tears of sorrow*    23 peering o'er: *rising above*

*Arth.* I do beseech you, madam, be content.

*Const.* If thou, that bid'st me be content, **wert**
   grim,
Ugly and slanderous to thy mother's womb,                    44
Full of unpleasing blots and sightless stains,
Lame, foolish, crooked, swart, prodigious,
Patch'd with foul moles and eye-offending marks,
I would not care, I then would be content;                    48
For then I should not love thee, no, nor thou
Become thy great birth, nor deserve a crown.
But thou art fair; and at thy birth, dear boy,
Nature and Fortune join'd to make thee great;                    52
Of Nature's gifts thou mayst with lilies boast
And with the half-blown rose. But Fortune, O!
She is corrupted, chang'd, and won from thee:
Sh' adulterates hourly with thine uncle John,                    56
And with her golden hand hath pluck'd on France
To tread down fair respect of sovereignty,
And made his majesty the bawd to theirs.
France is a bawd to Fortune and King John,                    60
That strumpet Fortune, that usurping John!
Tell me, thou fellow, is not France forsworn?
Envenom him with words, or get thee gone
And leave those woes alone which I alone                    64
Am bound to underbear.

*Sal.*            Pardon me, madam.
I may not go without you to the kings.

*Const.* Thou mayst, thou shalt; I will not go with
   thee.
I will instruct my sorrows to be proud;                    68
For grief is proud and makes his owner stoop.

42 content: *calm*                     44 slanderous: *a disgrace*
45 blots: *blemishes*    sightless: *unsightly*    stains: *disfigurements*
46 swart: *swarthy*    prodigious: *monstrous, misshapen*
56 adulterates: *commits adultery*
57 with her golden hand: *by bribes*    pluck'd on: *incited*
59 *Cf. n.*         63 Envenom: *poison*    65 underbear: *endure*

To me and to the state of my great grief
Let kings assemble; for my grief's so great
That no supporter but the huge firm earth            72
Can hold it up: here I and sorrows sit;
Here is my throne, bid kings come bow to it.

> [*Seats herself on the ground.*]

*Enter King John, France [King Philip], Dauphin
[Lewis], Blanch, Elinor, Philip [the Bastard],
Austria, Constance [and Attendants].*

*K. Phi.* 'Tis true, fair daughter, and this blessed
day
Ever in France shall be kept festival;            76
To solemnize this day the glorious sun
Stays in his course and plays the alchemist,
Turning with splendour of his precious eye
The meagre cloddy earth to glittering gold;            80
The yearly course that brings this day about
Shall never see it but a holy day.

*Const.* [*Rising.*] A wicked day, and not a holy
day!
What hath this day deserv'd? what hath it done            84
That it in golden letters should be set
Among the high tides in the calendar?
Nay, rather turn this day out of the week,
This day of shame, oppression, perjury.            88
Or, if it must stand still, let wives with child
Pray that their burthens may not fall this day,
Lest that their hopes prodigiously be cross'd:
But on this day let seamen fear no wrack;            92
No bargains break that are not this day made;

69-71 For grief . . . assemble; *cf. n.*            70 state: *seat of state*
76 festival: *like a feast-day*            78 plays the alchemist; *cf. n.*
80 meagre: *barren*            81 brings . . . about: *brings around*
86 high tides: *great festivals*            89 stand still: *still stand*
91 prodigiously: *by monstrous births*
92 But: *except*            wrack: *wreck*

This day all things begun come to ill end;
Yea, faith itself to hollow falsehood change!

*K. Phi.* By heaven, lady, you shall have no cause 96
To curse the fair proceedings of this day:
Have I not pawn'd to you my majesty?

*Const.* You have beguil'd me with a counterfeit
Resembling majesty, which, being touch'd and
    tried, 100
Proves valueless. You are forsworn, forsworn;
You came in arms to spill mine enemies' blood,
But now in arms you strengthen it with yours.
The grappling vigour and rough frown of war 104
Is cold in amity and painted peace,
And our oppression hath made up this league.
Arm, arm, you heavens, against these perjur'd kings!
A widow cries; be husband to me, heavens! 108
Let not the hours of this ungodly day
Wear out the day in peace; but, ere sunset,
Set armed discord 'twixt these perjur'd kings!
Hear me! O, hear me!

*Aust.*　　　　　　Lady Constance, peace! 112

*Const.* War! war! no peace! peace is to me a war.
O, Lymoges! O, Austria! thou dost shame
That bloody spoil: thou slave, thou wretch, thou
    coward!
Thou little valiant, great in villainy! 116
Thou ever strong upon the stronger side!
Thou Fortune's champion, that dost never fight
But when her humorous ladyship is by
To teach thee safety! thou art perjur'd too, 120
And sooth'st up greatness. What a fool art thou,
A ramping fool, to brag, and stamp and swear

---

98 pawn'd: *pledged*　　　　　　99 counterfeit: *false coin*
100 touch'd: *tested as with the touchstone*　　105 painted: *feigned*
106 oppression: *distress*　　　　　119 humorous: *fickle*
121 sooth'st up: *flatterest*　　122 ramping: *unrestrained*

Upon my party! Thou cold-blooded slave,
Hast thou not spoke like thunder on my side?    124
Been sworn my soldier? bidding me depend
Upon thy stars, thy fortune, and thy strength?
And dost thou now fall over to my foes?
Thou wear a lion's hide! doff it for shame,    128
And hang a calfskin on those recreant limbs.

*Aust.* O that a man should speak those words to
     me!

*Bast.* And hang a calfskin on those recreant limbs.

*Aust.* Thou dar'st not say so, villain, for thy life. 132

*Bast.* And hang a calfskin on those recreant limbs.

*K. John.* We like not this; thou dost forget thyself.

### Enter Pandulph.

*K. Phi.* Here comes the holy legate of the pope.

*Pand.* Hail, you anointed deputies of heaven!    136
To thee, King John, my holy errand is.
I Pandulph, of fair Milan cardinal,
And from Pope Innocent the legate here,
Do in his name religiously demand    140
Why thou against the church, our holy mother,
So wilfully dost spurn; and, force perforce,
Keep Stephen Langton, chosen Archbishop
Of Canterbury, from that holy see?    144
This, in our foresaid holy father's name,
Pope Innocent, I do demand of thee.

*K. John.* What earthy name to interrogatories
Can task the free breath of a sacred king?    148
Thou canst not, cardinal, devise a name
So slight, unworthy and ridiculous,

---

123 Upon my party: *on my side*            127 fall over: *desert*
129 recreant: *cowardly*                 140 religiously: *solemnly*
142 spurn: *oppose contemptuously*        force perforce: *by violent*
      constraint       143 Stephen Langton; *cf. n.*         147 *Cf. n.*
148 task: *compel*

To charge me to an answer, as the pope.
Tell him this tale; and from the mouth of England 152
Add thus much more: that no Italian priest
Shall tithe or toll in our dominions;
But as we under heaven are supreme head,
So under him that great supremacy,    156
Where we do reign, we will alone uphold,
Without th' assistance of a mortal hand.
So tell the pope, all reverence set apart
To him, and his usurp'd authority.    160

   *K. Phi.* Brother of England, you blaspheme in
   this.

   *K. John.* Though you and all the kings of Christen-
   dom
Are led so grossly by this meddling priest,
Dreading the curse that money may buy out;    164
And by the merit of vile gold, dross, dust,
Purchase corrupted pardon of a man,
Who in that sale sells pardon from himself;
Though you and all the rest, so grossly led,    168
This juggling witchcraft with revenue cherish;
Yet I alone, alone do me oppose
Against the pope, and count his friends my foes.

   *Pand.* Then, by the lawful power that I have,    172
Thou shalt stand curs'd and excommunicate;
And blessed shall he be that doth revolt
From his allegiance to a heretic;
And meritorious shall that hand be call'd,    176
Canonized and worshipp'd as a saint,
That takes away by any secret course
Thy hateful life.

---

151 charge: *command*    154 tithe or toll: *receive clerical revenues*
159 set apart: *discarded*    163 grossly: *stupidly*
164 buy out: *get rid of by a money payment*
166 corrupted: *bought by a bribe*    173 excommunicate; *cf. n.*
177 Canonized: *placed in the canon of saints*

   *Const.*        O lawful let it be
That I have room with Rome to curse awhile!   180
Good father cardinal, cry thou amen
To my keen curses; for without my wrong
There is no tongue hath power to curse him right.

   *Pand.* There's law and warrant, lady, for my
     curse.   184

   *Const.* And for mine too; when law can do no
     right,
Let it be lawful that law bar no wrong.
Law cannot give my child his kingdom here,
For he that holds his kingdom holds the law;   188
Therefore, since law itself is perfect wrong,
How can the law forbid my tongue to curse?

   *Pand.* Philip of France, on peril of a curse,
Let go the hand of that arch-heretic,   192
And raise the power of France upon his head,
Unless he do submit himself to Rome.

   *Eli.* Look'st thou pale, France? do not let go thy
     hand.

   *Const.* Look to that, devil, lest that France re-
     pent,   196
And by disjoining hands, hell lose a soul.

   *Aust.* King Philip, listen to the cardinal.

   *Bast.* And hang a calfskin on his recreant limbs.

   *Aust.* Well, ruffian, I must pocket up these
     wrongs,   200
Because—

   *Bast.*    Your breeches best may carry them.

   *K. John.* Philip, what sayst thou to the cardinal?

   *Const.* What should he say, but as the cardinal?

   *Lew.* Bethink you, father; for the difference   204
Is purchase of a heavy curse from Rome,

193 upon: *against*

Or the light loss of England for a friend:
Forgo the easier.

    *Blanch.*            That's the curse of Rome.

    *Const.* O Lewis, stand fast! the devil tempts thee here,      208
In likeness of a new untrimmed bride.

    *Blanch.* The Lady Constance speaks not from her faith,
But from her need.

    *Const.*          O! if thou grant my need,
Which only lives but by the death of faith,    212
That need must needs infer this principle,
That faith would live again by death of need.
O then, tread down my need, and faith mounts up;
Keep my need up, and faith is trodden down!    216

    *K. John.* The king is mov'd, and answers not to this.

    *Const.* O be remov'd from him, and answer well!

    *Aust.* Do so, King Philip; hang no more in doubt.

    *Bast.* Hang nothing but a calfskin, most sweet lout.    220

    *K. Phi.* I am perplex'd, and know not what to say.

    *Pand.* What canst thou say but will perplex thee more,
If thou stand excommunicate and curs'd?

    *K. Phi.* Good reverend father, make my person yours,    224
And tell me how you would bestow yourself.
This royal hand and mine are newly knit,
And the conjunction of our inward souls
Married in league, coupled and link'd together    228
With all religious strength of sacred vows;

---

207 Forgo the easier; *cf. n.*        209 new untrimmed bride; *cf. n.*
211-216 *Cf. n.*    224 make my person yours: *put yourself in my place*
225 bestow yourself: *behave yourself*

The latest breath that gave the sound of words
Was deep-sworn faith, peace, amity, true love
Between our kingdoms and our royal selves;          232
And even before this truce, but new before,
No longer than we well could wash our hands
To clap this royal bargain up of peace,
Heaven knows, they were besmear'd and over-
          stain'd                                    236
With slaughter's pencil, where revenge did paint
The fearful difference of incensed kings:
And shall these hands, so lately purg'd of blood,
So newly join'd in love, so strong in both,         240
Unyoke this seizure and this kind regreet?
Play fast and loose with faith? so jest with heaven,
Make such unconstant children of ourselves,
As now again to snatch our palm from palm,          244
Unswear faith sworn, and on the marriage-bed
Of smiling peace to march a bloody host,
And make a riot on the gentle brow
Of true sincerity?  O holy sir,                     248
My reverend father, let it not be so!
Out of your grace, devise, ordain, impose
Some gentle order; and then we shall be bless'd
To do your pleasure and continue friends.           252

     *Pand.* All form is formless, order orderless,
Save what is opposite to England's love.
Therefore to arms! be champion of our church,
Or let the church, our mother, breathe her curse,   256
A mother's curse, on her revolting son.
France, thou mayst hold a serpent by the tongue,

230 latest: *most recently made*          breath: *utterance*
231 deep-sworn: *solemnly sworn*     233 new: *recently*     233, 234 *Cf. n.*
235 clap . . . up: *to strike hands reciprocally in token of a bargain*
238 difference: *quarrel*
241 Unyoke: *disjoin*          seizure: *clasp*          regreet: *greeting*
242 Play fast and loose; *cf. n.*          243 unconstant: *changeable*
250 ordain: *decree*                      253 form: *orderly arrangement*

A cased lion by the mortal paw,
A fasting tiger safer by the tooth,                          260
Than keep in peace that hand which thou dost hold.
  *K. Phi.* I may disjoin my hand, but not my faith.
  *Pand.* So mak'st thou faith an enemy to faith;
And like a civil war set'st oath to oath,                    264
Thy tongue against thy tongue. O! let thy vow
First made to heaven, first be to heaven perform'd,
That is, to be the champion of our church.
What since thou swor'st is sworn against thyself             268
And may not be performed by thyself;
For that which thou hast sworn to do amiss
Is not amiss when it is truly done;
And being not done, where doing tends to ill,               272
The truth is then most done not doing it.
The better act of purposes mistook
Is to mistake again; though indirect,
Yet indirection thereby grows direct,                        276
And falsehood falsehood cures, as fire cools fire
Within the scorched veins of one new burn'd.
It is religion that doth make vows kept,
But thou hast sworn against religion:                       280
By what thou swear'st, against the thing thou
    swear'st,
And mak'st an oath the surety for thy truth
Against an oath; the truth thou art unsure
To swear, swears only not to be forsworn;                   284
Else what a mockery should it be to swear!
But thou dost swear only to be forsworn;
And most forsworn, to keep what thou dost swear.
Therefore thy later vows against thy first                  288
Is in thyself rebellion to thyself;

259 A cased lion; *cf. n.*    mortal: *deadly*
264 set'st . . . to: *pittest . . . against*        270-273 *Cf. n.*
274 act: *execution*      275, 276 though . . . direct; *cf. n.*
276 indirection: *irregular or unjust means*     279-287 *Cf. n.*

And better conquest never canst thou make
Than arm thy constant and thy nobler parts
Against these giddy loose suggestions:                292
Upon which better part our prayers come in,
If thou vouchsafe them. But, if not, then know
The peril of our curses light on thee
So heavy as thou shalt not shake them off,            296
But in despair die under their black weight.

   *Aust.* Rebellion, flat rebellion!

   *Bast.*              Will 't not be?
Will not a calfskin stop that mouth of thine?

   *Lew.* Father, to arms!

   *Blanch.*         Upon thy wedding-day?  300
Against the blood that thou hast married?
What! shall our feast be kept with slaughter'd men?
Shall braying trumpets and loud churlish drums,
Clamours of hell, be measures to our pomp?           304
O husband, hear me! ay, alack! how new
Is 'husband' in my mouth! Even for that name,
Which till this time my tongue did ne'er pronounce,
Upon my knee I beg, go not to arms                    308
Against mine uncle.

   *Const.*        O! upon my knee,
Made hard with kneeling, I do pray to thee,
Thou virtuous Dauphin, alter not the doom
Forethought by heaven.                                312

   *Blanch.* Now shall I see thy love: what motive
      may
Be stronger with thee than the name of wife?

   *Const.* That which upholdeth him that thee up-
      holds,

---

291 arm: *by arming*         292 suggestions: *temptations*
293 Upon which better part: *in support of which better side*
296 as: *that*   298 flat: *downright*   301 blood: *blood-relationship*
304 measures: *melodies*
312 Forethought: *predestined*       311 doom: *judgment*
                    313 motive: *incitement to action*

His honour. O thine honour, Lewis, thine honour! 316

  *Lew.* I muse your majesty doth seem so cold,

When such profound respects do pull you on.

  *Pand.* I will denounce a curse upon his head.

  *K. Phi.* Thou shalt not need. England, I will **fall**
from thee.    320

  *Const.* O fair return of banish'd majesty!

  *Eli.* O foul revolt of French inconstancy!

  *K. John.* France, thou shalt rue this hour within
this hour.

  *Bast.* Old Time the clock-setter, that bald sexton
Time,    324

Is it as he will? well then, France shall rue.

  *Blanch.* The sun's o'ercast with blood; fair **day,**
adieu!

Which is the side that I must go withal?

I am with both: each army hath a hand;    328

And in their rage, I having hold of both,

They whirl asunder and dismember me.

Husband, I cannot pray that thou mayst win;

Uncle, I needs must pray that thou mayst lose;    332

Father, I may not wish the fortune thine;

Grandam, I will not wish thy wishes thrive:

Whoever wins, on that side shall I lose;

Assured loss before the match be play'd.    336

  *Lew.* Lady, with me, with me thy fortune lies.

  *Blanch.* There where my fortune lives, there my life
dies.

  *K. John.* Cousin, go draw our puissance together.

                             [*Exit Bastard.*]

France, I am burn'd up with inflaming wrath;    340

---

317 muse: *wonder*     318 profound respects: *weighty considerations*
319 denounce: *proclaim*                    320 fall from: *forsake*
324 Old Time the clock-setter; *cf. n.*         327 withal: *with*
339 Cousin: *kinsman*     draw: *gather*     puissance: *armed force*

A rage whose heat hath this condition,
That nothing can allay, nothing but blood,
The blood, and dearest-valu'd blood, of France.

    *K. Phi.* Thy rage shall burn thee up, and thou
        shalt turn                  344
To ashes, ere our blood shall quench that fire:
Look to thyself, thou art in jeopardy.

    *K. John.* No more than he that threats.  To arms
        let's hie!

                                    *Exeunt.*


## Scene Two

### [*The Same.    Plains near Angiers*]

*Alarums, excursions.    Enter Bastard, with Austria's
head.*

    *Bast.* Now, by my life, this day grows wondrous
        hot;
Some airy devil hovers in the sky
And pours down mischief.  Austria's head lie there,
While Philip breathes.                      4

### *Enter John, Arthur, Hubert.*

    *K. John.* Hubert, keep this boy.  Philip, make up;
My mother is assailed in our tent,
And ta'en, I fear.

    *Bast.*           My lord, I rescu'd her;
Her highness is in safety, fear you not.        8
But on, my liege; for very little pains
Will bring this labour to a happy end.

                                       *Exit.*

---

341 condition: *quality*    2 airy devil; *cf. n.*    4 breathes: *takes breath*
5 Philip; *cf. n.*      make up: *push forward*

## Scene Three

### [*The Same*]

*Alarums, excursions, retreat. Enter John, Elinor,
Arthur, Bastard, Hubert, Lords.*

*K. John.* [*To Elinor.*] So shall it be; your grace
shall stay behind
So strongly guarded. [*To Arthur.*] Cousin, look not
sad:
Thy grandam loves thee; and thy uncle will
As dear be to thee as thy father was.　　　　　4
　*Arth.* O this will make my mother die with grief!
　*K. John.* [*To the Bastard.*] Cousin, away for Eng-
land! haste before;
And, ere our coming, see thou shake the bags
Of hoarding abbots; imprison'd angels　　　　　8
Set at liberty; the fat ribs of peace
Must by the hungry now be fed upon;
Use our commission in his utmost force.
　*Bast.* Bell, book, and candle shall not drive me
back　　　　　12
When gold and silver becks me to come on.
I leave your highness. Grandam, I will pray,—
If ever I remember to be holy,—
For your fair safety; so I kiss your hand.　　　　16
　*Eli.* Farewell, gentle cousin.
　*K. John.*　　　　　Coz, farewell.
　　　　　　　　　　　[*Exit Bastard.*]
　*Eli.* Come hither, little kinsman; hark, a word.
　　　　　　　　　[*She takes Arthur aside.*]
　*K. John.* Come hither, Hubert. O my gentle Hu-
bert,

6 before: *in front*　　8, 9 imprison'd . . . liberty; *cf. n.*
12 Bell, book, and candle; *cf. n.*　13 becks: *beckons*　18 *Cf. n.*

We owe thee much! within this wall of flesh          20
There is a soul counts thee her creditor,
And with advantage means to pay thy love;
And, my good friend, thy voluntary oath
Lives in this bosom, dearly cherished.               24
Give me thy hand.   I had a thing to say,
But I will fit it with some better tune.
By heaven, Hubert, I am almost asham'd
To say what good respect I have of thee.             28

    *Hub.* I am much bounden to your majesty.

    *K. John.* Good friend, thou hast no cause to say so
      yet;
But thou shalt have; and creep time ne'er so slow,
Yet it shall come for me to do thee good.            32
I had a thing to say, but let it go.
The sun is in the heaven, and the proud day,
Attended with the pleasures of the world,
Is all too wanton and too full of gawds              36
To give me audience.   If the midnight bell
Did, with his iron tongue and brazen mouth,
Sound on into the drowsy race of night;
If this same were a churchyard where we stand,       40
And thou possessed with a thousand wrongs;
Or if that surly spirit, melancholy,
Had bak'd thy blood and made it heavy, thick,
Which else runs tickling up and down the veins,      44
Making that idiot, laughter, keep men's eyes
And strain their cheeks to idle merriment,
A passion hateful to my purposes;
Or if that thou couldst see me without eyes,         48
Hear me without thine ears, and make reply
Without a tongue, using conceit alone,

22 advantage: *interest*      28 respect: *esteem*      29 bounden: *obliged*
36 wanton: *merry*      gawds: *playthings*                      39 *Cf. n.*
45 keep: *occupy*                      47 passion: *an emotional state (mirth)*
50 conceit: *understanding*

Without eyes, ears, and harmful sound of words;
Then, in despite of brooded watchful day,                52
I would into thy bosom pour my thoughts.
But ah! I will not; yet I love thee well;
And, by my troth, I think thou lov'st me well.

   *Hub.* So well, that what you bid me undertake,   56
Though that my death were adjunct to my act,
By heaven, I would do it.

   *K. John.*         Do not I know thou wouldst?
Good Hubert! Hubert, Hubert, throw thine eye
On yon young boy: I'll tell thee what, my friend,   60
He is a very serpent in my way;
And wheresoe'er this foot of mine doth tread
He lies before me. Dost thou understand me?
Thou art his keeper.

   *Hub.*       And I'll keep him so   64
That he shall not offend your majesty.

   *K. John.* Death.

   *Hub.*     My lord?

   *K. John.*      A grave.

   *Hub.*          He shall not live.

   *K. John.*            Enough.
I could be merry now. Hubert, I love thee;
Well, I'll not say what I intend for thee.           68
Remember. Madam, fare you well.
I'll send those powers o'er to your majesty.

   *Eli.* My blessing go with thee!

   *K. John.*         For England, cousin, go.
Hubert shall be your man, attend on you           72
With all true duty. On toward Calais, ho!

                        *Exeunt.*

---

52 brooded: *having a brood to watch over*      55 troth: *faith*
57 adjunct to: *connected with*           59 throw: *direct*
60 what: *something*                70 powers: *troops*

## Scene Four

*[The Same.   The French King's Tent]*

*Enter France, Dauphin, Pandulph, Attendants.*

*K. Phi.* So, by a roaring tempest on the flood,
A whole armado of convicted sail
Is scatter'd and disjoin'd from fellowship.

   *Pand.* Courage and comfort! all shall yet go well.  4

   *K. Phi.* What can go well when we have run so
     ill?
Are we not beaten?  Is not Angiers lost?
Arthur ta'en prisoner? divers dear friends slain?
And bloody England into England gone,                        8
O'erbearing interruption, spite of France?

   *Lew.* What he hath won that hath he fortified.
So hot a speed with such advice dispos'd,
Such temperate order in so fierce a cause,                    12
Doth want example.   Who hath read or heard
Of any kindred action like to this?

   *K. Phi.* Well could I bear that England had this
     praise,
So we could find some pattern of our shame.                   16

*Enter Constance.*

Look, who comes here! a grave unto a soul,
Holding th' eternal spirit, against her will,
In the vile prison of afflicted breath.
I prithee, lady, go away with me.                             20

   *Const.* Lo, now! now see the issue of your peace!

---

1 flood: *sea*     2 armado: *fleet of war*     convicted: *defeated*
3 fellowship: *companionship*              6, 7 *Cf. n.*
9 interruption: *resistance*     spite of: *in spite of*
11 advice: *consideration*     dispos'd: *regulated*
13 example: *parallel case in the past*     14 kindred: *cognate*
16 So: *if*     pattern: *precedent*     19 breath: *life*

    *K. Phi.* Patience, good lady! comfort, gentle Con-
      stance!

    *Const.* No, I defy all counsel, all redress,
But that which ends all counsel, true redress,    24
Death, death; O, amiable, lovely death!
Thou odoriferous stench! sound rottenness!
Arise forth from the couch of lasting night,
Thou hate and terror to prosperity,    28
And I will kiss thy detestable bones,
And put my eyeballs in thy vaulty brows,
And ring these fingers with thy household worms,
And stop this gap of breath with fulsome dust,    32
And be a carrion monster like thyself.
Come, grin on me; and I will think thou smil'st
And buss thee as thy wife! Misery's love,
O, come to me!

    *K. Phi.*         O fair affliction, peace!    36

    *Const.* No, no, I will not, having breath to cry.
O that my tongue were in the thunder's mouth!
Then with a passion would I shake the world,
And rouse from sleep that fell anatomy    40
Which cannot hear a lady's feeble voice,
Which scorns a modern invocation.

    *Pand.* Lady, you utter madness and not sorrow.

    *Const.* Thou art [not] holy to belie me so;    44
I am not mad: this hair I tear is mine;
My name is Constance; I was Geoffrey's wife;
Young Arthur is my son, and he is lost!
I am not mad: I would to heaven I were!    48
For then 'tis like I should forget myself.
O, if I could, what grief should I forget!
Preach some philosophy to make me mad,

---

23 defy: *reject*     27 lasting: *everlasting*     30 vaulty: *arched*
32 gap of breath: *mouth*     fulsome: *physically disgusting*
35 buss: *kiss*                 40 fell anatomy: *cruel skeleton*
42 modern: *everyday*     44 *Cf. n.*     49 like: *probable*

And thou shalt be canoniz'd, Cardinal.                    52
For being not mad but sensible of grief,
My reasonable part produces reason
How I may be deliver'd of these woes,
And teaches me to kill or hang myself.                    56
If I were mad, I should forget my son,
Or madly think a babe of clouts were he.
I am not mad: too well, too well I feel
The different plague of each calamity.                    60

   *K. Phi.* Bind up those tresses.  O! what love I
     note
In the fair multitude of those her hairs!
Where but by chance a silver drop hath fallen,
Even to that drop ten thousand wiry friends          64
Do glue themselves in sociable grief;
Like true, inseparable, faithful loves,
Sticking together in calamity.

   *Const.* To England, if you will.
   *K. Phi.*                            Bind up your hairs.  68
   *Const.* Yes, that I will; and wherefore will I do it?
I tore them from their bonds, and cried aloud:
'O that these hands could so redeem my son,
As they have given these hairs their liberty!'          72
But now I envy at their liberty,
And will again commit them to their bonds,
Because my poor child is a prisoner.
And, Father Cardinal, I have heard you say               76
That we shall see and know our friends in heaven.
If that be true, I shall see my boy again;
For since the birth of Cain, the first male child,
To him that did but yesterday suspire,                   80
There was not such a gracious creature born.

---

53 sensible of: *capable of*        58 babe of clouts: *rag-doll*
64 wiry friends; *cf. n.*        65 sociable: *sympathetic*
68 To England; *cf. n.*        73 envy: *feel jealousy*
80 suspire: *draw breath*        81 gracious: *lovely*

But now will canker-sorrow eat my bud
And chase the native beauty from his cheek,
And he will look as hollow as a ghost,                84
As dim and meagre as an ague's fit,
And so he'll die; and, rising so again,
When I shall meet him in the court of heaven
I shall not know him.   Therefore never, never        88
Must I behold my pretty Arthur more.
   *Pand.* You hold too heinous a respect of grief.
   *Const.* He 'talks to me, that never had a son.
   *K. Phi.* You are as fond of grief as of your child. 92
   *Const.* Grief fills the room up of my absent **child,**
Lies in his bed, walks up and down with me,
Puts on his pretty looks, repeats his words,
Remembers me of all his gracious parts,               96
Stuffs out his vacant garments with his form:
Then have I reason to be fond of grief.
Fare you well: had you such a loss as I,
I could give better comfort than you do.              100
I will not keep this form upon my head,
When there is such disorder in my wit.
O Lord! my boy, my Arthur, my fair son!
My life, my joy, my food, my all the world!           104
My widow-comfort, and my sorrows' cure!

                                         *Exit.*
   *K. Phi.* I fear some outrage, and I'll follow her.
                                         *Exit.*
   *Lew.* There's nothing in this world can make me
    joy:
Life is as tedious as a twice-told tale,              108
Vexing the dull ear of a drowsy man;
And bitter shame hath spoil'd the sweet world's taste,

82 canker: *like a canker worm*          85 dim: *lustreless*
90 hold: *entertain*   respect: *opinion*      92 fond: *infatuated*
96 Remembers: *reminds*      101 form: *orderly arrangement*
102 wit: *mind*

That it yields nought but shame and bitterness.

    *Pand.* Before the curing of a strong disease,    112
Even in the instant of repair and health,
The fit is strongest: evils that take leave,
On their departure most of all show evil.
What have you lost by losing of this day?    116

    *Lew.* All days of glory, joy, and happiness.

    *Pand.* If you had won it, certainly you had.
No, no; when Fortune means to men most good,
She looks upon them with a threat'ning eye.    120
'Tis strange to think how much King John hath lost
In this which he accounts so clearly won.
Are not you griev'd that Arthur is his prisoner?

    *Lew.* As heartily as he is glad he hath him.    124

    *Pand.* Your mind is all as youthful as your blood.
Now hear me speak with a prophetic spirit;
For even the breath of what I mean to speak
Shall blow each dust, each straw, each little rub,    128
Out of the path which shall directly lead
Thy foot to England's throne; and therefore mark.
John hath seiz'd Arthur; and it cannot be,
That, whiles warm life plays in that infant's veins, 132
The misplac'd John should entertain an hour,
One minute, nay, one quiet breath of rest.
A sceptre snatch'd with an unruly hand
Must be as boisterously maintain'd as gain'd;    136
And he that stands upon a slippery place
Makes nice of no vile hold to stay him up:
That John may stand, then Arthur needs must fall;
So be it, for it cannot be but so.    140

    *Lew.* But what shall I gain by young Arthur's fall?

---

113 repair: *restoration*                116 day: *day of battle*
128 dust: *grain of dust*    rub: *obstacle*
133 misplac'd: *usurping the place of another*    entertain: *spend*
138 Makes nice of: *is scrupulous about*    hold: *grasp*
    stay . . . up: *support*

*Pand.* You, in the right of Lady Blanch your wife,
May then make all the claim that Arthur did.

*Lew.* And lose it, life and all, as Arthur did.     144

*Pand.* How green you are and fresh in this old
     world!
John lays you plots; the times conspire with you;
For he that steeps his safety in true blood
Shall find but bloody safety and untrue.     148
This act so evilly borne shall cool the hearts
Of all his people and freeze up their zeal,
That none so small advantage shall step forth
To check his reign, but they will cherish it;     152
No natural exhalation in the sky,
No scope of nature, no distemper'd day,
No common wind, no customed event,
But they will pluck away his natural cause     156
And call them meteors, prodigies, and signs,
Abortives, presages, and tongues of heaven,
Plainly denouncing vengeance upon John.

*Lew.* May be he will not touch young Arthur's
     life,     160
But hold himself safe in his prisonment.

*Pand.* O, sir, when he shall hear of your approach,
If that young Arthur be not gone already,
Even at that news he dies; and then the hearts     164
Of all his people shall revolt from him
And kiss the lips of unacquainted change,
And pick strong matter of revolt and wrath
Out of the bloody fingers' ends of John.     168

---

145 green: *inexperienced*            146 you: *for your advantage*
147, 148 *Cf. n.*      149 so evilly borne: *carried through so wickedly*
151 advantage: *opportunity*           153 exhalation: *meteor*
154 scope of nature: *circumstance within the limits of nature's opera-*
     *tions*         distemper'd day: *day of bad weather*
155 customed: *customary*             156 his: *its*
158 Abortives: *untimely births*      161 prisonment: *captivity*
166 unacquainted: *unfamiliar*          167, 168 *Cf. n.*

Methinks I see this hurly all on foot;
And, O! what better matter breeds for you
Than I have nam'd! The bastard Faulconbridge
Is now in England, ransacking the church,                172
Offending charity. If but a dozen French
Were there in arms, they would be as a call
To train ten thousand English to their side;
Or as a little snow, tumbled about,                      176
Anon becomes a mountain. O noble Dauphin,
Go with me to the king. 'Tis wonderful
What may be wrought out of their discontent,
Now that their souls are topful of offence.              180
For England go; I will whet on the king.

    *Lew.* Strong reasons make strong actions. Let us
      go;
If you say ay, the king will not say no.

                        *Exeunt.*


# ACT FOURTH

## Scene One

*[Northampton. A Room in the Castle]*

*Enter Hubert and Executioners.*

    *Hub.* Heat me these irons hot; and look thou stand
Within the arras. When I strike my foot
Upon the bosom of the ground, rush forth,
And bind the boy which you shall find with me          4
Fast to the chair. Be heedful. Hence, and watch.

---

169 hurly: *commotion*   on foot: *started*   172 ransacking: *pillaging*
173 charity: *good will*     174 call: *decoy-bird*     175 train: *lure*
177 Anon: *straightway*   180 topful of offence: *brimful of displeasure*
181 whet on: *instigate*     2 arras; *cf. n.*     3 bosom: *surface*

[1] *Exec.* I hope your warrant will bear out the
deed.

*Hub.* Uncleanly scruples! fear not you: look to 't.
[*Exeunt Executioners.*]

Young lad, come forth; I have to say with you.    8

*Enter Arthur.*

*Arth.* Good morrow, Hubert.

*Hub.*                    Good morrow, little prince.

*Arth.* As little prince, having so great a title
To be more prince, as may be.  You are sad.

*Hub.* Indeed, I have been merrier.

*Arth.*                    Mercy on me! 12

Methinks nobody should be sad but I.
Yet I remember, when I was in France,
Young gentlemen would be as sad as night,
Only for wantonness.  By my christendom,    16
So I were out of prison and kept sheep,
I should be as merry as the day is long;
And so I would be here, but that I doubt
My uncle practises more harm to me.    20
He is afraid of me, and I of him.
Is it my fault that I was Geoffrey's son?
No, indeed, is 't not; and I would to heaven
I were your son, so you would love me, Hubert.    24

*Hub.* [*Aside.*] If I talk to him, with his innocent
prate
He will awake my mercy which lies dead;
Therefore I will be sudden and dispatch.

*Arth.* Are you sick, Hubert? you look pale to-
day.    28

6 bear out: *support*          7 fear not you: *do not be frightened*
16 wantonness: *sportiveness*          christendom: *Christianity*
17 So: *provided that*    19 doubt: *fear*    20 practises: *schemes*
25 prate: *prattle*    27 sudden: *quick*    dispatch: *make haste*

In sooth, I would you were a little sick,

That I might sit all night and watch with you.

I warrant I love you more than you do me.

   *Hub.* [*Aside.*] His words do take possession of my
      bosom.                              32

Read here, young Arthur.       [*Showing a paper.*]
                      [*Aside.*] How now, foolish rheum!

Turning dispiteous torture out of door!

I must be brief, lest resolution drop

Out at mine eyes in tender womanish tears.      36

Can you not read it? is it not fair writ?

   *Arth.* Too fairly, Hubert, for so foul effect.

Must you with hot irons burn out both mine eyes?

   *Hub.* Young boy, I must.

   *Arth.*              And will you?

   *Hub.*                    And I will. 40

   *Arth.* Have you the heart? When your head did but
      ache,

I knit my handkercher about your brows,—

The best I had, a princess wrought it me,—

And I did never ask it you again;      44

And with my hand at midnight held your head,

And like the watchful minutes to the hour,

Still and anon cheer'd up the heavy time,

Saying, 'What lack you?' and 'Where lies your
      grief?'                              48

Or 'What good love may I perform for you?'

Many a poor man's son would have lien still,

And ne'er have spoke a loving word to you;

But you at your sick-service had a prince.      52

---

29 sooth: *truth*    34 dispiteous: *pitiless*    37 fair writ: *clearly written*
38 effect: *purpose*              42 handkercher: *handkerchief*
43 wrought it me: *worked it for me*
46 watchful minutes to the hour: *minutes that watch the progress of
    the hour*
47 Still and anon: *ever and anon*       heavy: *dreary*
49 love: *act of love*    50 lien: *lain*    52 sick-service: *service when sick*

Nay, you may think my love was crafty love,
And call it cunning; do and if you will.
If heaven be pleas'd that you must use me ill,
Why then you must.  Will you put out mine eyes?    56
These eyes that never did nor never shall
So much as frown on you?
    *Hub.*             I have sworn to do it;
And with hot irons must I burn them out.
    *Arth.* Ah! none but in this iron age would do it!    60
The iron of itself, though heat red-hot,
Approaching near these eyes, would drink my tears
And quench this fiery indignation
Even in the matter of mine innocence;            64
Nay, after that, consume away in rust,
But for containing fire to harm mine eye.
Are you more stubborn-hard than hammer'd iron?
And if an angel should have come to me        68
And told me Hubert should put out mine eyes,
I would not have believ'd him,—no tongue but Hubert's.
    *Hub.* [*Stamps.*] Come forth.

    [*Re-enter Executioners, with a cord, irons, &c.*]

Do as I bid you do.                           72
    *Arth.* O! save me, Hubert, save me! my eyes are out
Even with the fierce looks of these bloody men.
    *Hub.* Give me the iron, I say, and bind him here.
    *Arth.* Alas! what need you be so boist'rous-rough? 76
I will not struggle; I will stand stone still.
For heaven sake, Hubert, let me not be bound!
Nay, hear me, Hubert!  Drive these men away,

53 crafty: *feigned*      54 cunning: *craft*      60 iron: *merciless*
61 heat: *heated*
66 But: *merely*      for containing: *because it contained*
76 what: *why*

And I will sit as quiet as a lamb;                              80
I will not stir, nor wince, nor speak a word,
Nor look upon the iron angerly.
Thrust but these men away, and I'll forgive you,
Whatever torment you do put me to.                              84
   *Hub.* Go, stand within; let me alone with him.
   [*1*] *Exec.* I am best pleas'd to be from such a
deed.                              [*Exeunt Executioners.*]
   *Arth.* Alas! I then have chid away my friend;
He hath a stern look, but a gentle heart.                       88
Let him come back, that his compassion may
Give life to yours.
   *Hub.*       Come, boy, prepare yourself.
   *Arth.* Is there no remedy?
   *Hub.*          None, but to lose your eyes.
   *Arth.* O heaven! that there were but a moth in
     yours,                              92
A grain, a dust, a gnat, a wandering hair,
Any annoyance in that precious sense.
Then feeling what small things are boisterous there,
Your vile intent must needs seem horrible.                      96
   *Hub.* Is this your promise? go to, hold your tongue.
   *Arth.* Hubert, the utterance of a brace of tongues
Must needs want pleading for a pair of eyes.
Let me not hold my tongue; let me not, Hubert;                 100
Or, Hubert, if you will, cut out my tongue,
So I may keep mine eyes.  O! spare mine eyes,
Though to no use but still to look on you!
Lo! by my troth, the instrument is cold                        104
And would not harm me.
   *Hub.*      I can heat it, boy.

82 angerly: *angrily*    85 let . . . alone: *trust*    86 from: *clear of*
92 moth: *minute particle of anything, a mote*
95 boisterous: *causing a great commotion*    97 go to: *come, no more*
98, 99 *Cf. n.*
                                        104 troth: *faith*

*Arth.* No, in good sooth; the fire is dead with
   grief,
Being create for comfort, to be us'd
In undeserv'd extremes: see else yourself.          108
There is no malice in this burning coal;
The breath of heaven hath blown his spirit out
And strew'd repentant ashes on his head.
   *Hub.* But with my breath I can revive it, boy.   112
   *Arth.* And if you do, you will but make it blush
And glow with shame of your proceedings, Hubert.
Nay, it perchance will sparkle in your eyes;
And like a dog that is compell'd to fight,          116
Snatch at his master that doth tarre him on.
All things that you should use to do me wrong
Deny their office: only you do lack
That mercy which fierce fire and iron extends,      120
Creatures of note for mercy-lacking uses.
   *Hub.* Well, see to live; I will not touch thine eye
For all the treasure that thine uncle owes.
Yet am I sworn and I did purpose, boy,              124
With this same very iron to burn them out.
   *Arth.* O! now you look like Hubert; all this while
You were disguis'd.
   *Hub.*               Peace! no more. Adieu.
Your uncle must not know but you are dead;          128
I'll fill these dogged spies with false reports.
And, pretty child, sleep doubtless and secure,
That Hubert for the wealth of all the world
Will not offend thee.
   *Arth.*               O heaven! I thank you, Hubert. 132

---

107 create: *created*
108 extremes: *extremities*        else: *if it is not believed*
110 spirit: *vital energy*    111 repentant: *used in sign of repentance*
115 sparkle: *throw out sparks*              117 tarre: *provoke*
119 Deny their office: *refuse their proper function*    120 extends: *show*
121 of note: *noted*    122 Well, see to live; *cf. n.*    128 but: *that . . . not*
130 doubtless: *fearless*        secure: *without anxiety*

*Hub.* Silence! no more! go closely in with me:
Much danger do I undergo for thee.

*Exeunt.*

### Scene Two

[*The Same. A Room of State in the Palace*]

*Enter* [*King*] *John,* [*crowned*], *Pembroke, Salisbury,
and other Lords.* [*The King takes his state.*]

*K. John.* Here once again we sit, once again
    crown'd,
And look'd upon, I hope, with cheerful eyes.

*Pem.* This 'once again,' but that your highness
    pleas'd,
Was once superfluous: you were crown'd before,          4
And that high royalty was ne'er pluck'd off,
The faiths of men ne'er stained with revolt;
Fresh expectation troubled not the land
With any long'd for change or better state.             8

*Sal.* Therefore, to be possess'd with double pomp,
To guard a title that was rich before,
To gild refined gold, to paint the lily,
To throw a perfume on the violet,                       12
To smooth the ice, or add another hue
Unto the rainbow, or with taper-light
To seek the beauteous eye of heaven to garnish,
Is wasteful and ridiculous excess.                      16

*Pem.* But that your royal pleasure must be done,
This act is as an ancient tale new told,
And in the last repeating troublesome,
Being urged at a time unseasonable.                     20

*Sal.* In this the antique and well noted face

---

133 closely: *secretly*
6 stained: *corrupted*
10 guard: *ornament with borders, trim*
15 eye of heaven: *sun*    garnish: *dress*

4 superfluous: *more than enough*
7 expectation: *excited craving*

Of plain old form is much disfigured;
And, like a shifted wind unto a sail,
It makes the course of thoughts to fetch about,   24
Startles and frights consideration,
Makes sound opinion sick and truth suspected,
For putting on so new a fashion'd robe.

   *Pem.* When workmen strive to do better than
      well,   28
They do confound their skill in covetousness;
And oftentimes excusing of a fault
Doth make the fault the worse by the excuse:
As patches set upon a little breach   32
Discredit more in hiding of the fault
Than did the fault before it was so patch'd.

   *Sal.* To this effect, before you were new-crown'd,
We breath'd our counsel, but it pleas'd your high-
      ness   36
To overbear it, and we are all well pleas'd;
Since all and every part of what we would
Doth make a stand at what your highness will.

   *K. John.* Some reasons of this double coronation  40
I have possess'd you with and think them strong;
And more, more strong, when lesser is my fear,
I shall indue you with.   Meantime but ask
What you would have reform'd that is not well,   44
And well shall you perceive how willingly
I will both hear and grant you your requests.

   *Pem.* Then I, as one that am the tongue of these
To sound the purposes of all their hearts,   48
Both for myself and them,—but, chief of all,

23 a shifted wind: *a change of wind*
24 fetch about: *alter their direction*
25 consideration: *thoughtfulness*
29 confound: *ruin*
32 breach: *rent*   33 fault: *defect*   36 breath'd: *spoke*
37 overbear: *overrule*   39 make a stand at: *go no further than*
41 possess'd you with: *informed you of*   43 indue: *furnish*
48 sound: *utter*

Your safety, for the which myself and them
Bend their best studies,—heartily request
Th' enfranchisement of Arthur; whose restraint        52
Doth move the murmuring lips of discontent
To break into this dangerous argument:
If what in rest you have in right you hold,
Why then your fears, which, as they say, attend        56
The steps of wrong, should move you to mew up
Your tender kinsman, and to choke his days
With barbarous ignorance, and deny his youth
The rich advantage of good exercise.                  60
That the time's enemies may not have this
To grace occasions, let it be our suit
That you have bid us ask, his liberty;
Which for our goods we do no further ask              64
Than whereupon our weal, on you depending,
Counts it your weal he have his liberty.

*Enter Hubert.*

*K. John.* Let it be so; I do commit his youth
To your direction.   Hubert, what news with you?   68
                                    [*Taking him apart.*]
*Pem.* This is the man should do the bloody deed;
He show'd his warrant to a friend of mine.
The image of a wicked heinous fault
Lives in his eye; that close aspect of his            72
Does show the mood of a much troubled breast;
And I do fearfully believe 'tis done,

50 them: *i.e. they*      51 Bend: *direct*        studies: *diligent endeavors*
52 enfranchisement: *release from prison*
55 *If you rightfully hold what you are peaceably possessed of*
57 mew up: *shut up*                          60 exercise: *training*
61 time's: *present state of affairs'*
62 grace: *lend credit to*        occasions: *opportunities for fault-finding*
64 goods: *our own good*
65 whereupon: *in consequence of the fact that*        weal: *welfare*
71 image: *semblance*
72 Lives: *is alive*        close aspect: *secret expression*
74 fearfully believe: *fear and believe*

What we so fear'd he had a charge to do.

   *Sal.* The colour of the king doth come and go    **76**
Between his purpose and his conscience,
Like heralds 'twixt two dreadful battles set:
His passion is so ripe it needs must break.

   *Pem.* And when it breaks, I fear will issue thence **80**
The foul corruption of a sweet child's death.

   *K. John.* We cannot hold mortality's strong hand:
Good lords, although my will to give is living,
The suit which you demand is gone and dead:    **84**
He tells us Arthur is deceas'd to-night.

   *Sal.* Indeed we fear'd his sickness was past cure.

   *Pem.* Indeed we heard how near his death he was,
Before the child himself felt he was sick.    **88**
This must be answer'd, either here or hence.

   *K. John.* Why do you bend such solemn brows on
    me?
Think you I bear the shears of destiny?
Have I commandment on the pulse of life?    **92**

   *Sal.* It is apparent foul play; and 'tis shame
That greatness should so grossly offer it.
So thrive it in your game! and so, farewell.

   *Pem.* Stay yet, Lord Salisbury; I'll go with thee, **96**
And find th' inheritance of this poor child,
His little kingdom of a forced grave.
That blood which ow'd the breadth of all this isle,
Three foot of it doth hold; bad world the while!    **100**
This must not be thus borne; this will break out
To all our sorrows, and ere long, I doubt.

                       *Exeunt* [*Lords*].

75 charge: *order*    78 battles: *armies arrayed for battle*    set: *placed*
79 break: *break open (as a boil or tumor)*    82 mortality's: *death's*
89 answer'd: *atoned for*    hence: *in the next world*
90 bend . . . solemn brows: *scowl*    91 shears of destiny; *cf. n.*
94 grossly: *flagrantly*    offer: *venture*
98 forced: *violent*    99 blood: *life*
100 bad world the while!: *a bad world where such things happen!*
101 borne: *put up with*    102 all our: *of us all*

*K. John.* They burn in indignation.  I repent.

*Enter Mes[senger].*

There is no sure foundation set on blood,                    104
No certain life achiev'd by others' death.
A fearful eye thou hast; where is that blood
That I have seen inhabit in those cheeks?
So foul a sky clears not without a storm:                    108
Pour down thy weather.  How goes all in France?

   *Mess.* From France to England.  Never such a
     power
For any foreign preparation
Was levied in the body of a land.                            112
The copy of your speed is learn'd by them;
For when you should be told they do prepare,
The tidings comes that they are all arriv'd.

   *K. John.* O! where hath our intelligence been
     drunk?                                                116
Where hath it slept?  Where is my mother's care,
That such an army could be drawn in France,
And she not hear of it?

   *Mess.*            My liege, her ear
Is stopp'd with dust; the first of April died                120
Your noble mother; and, as I hear, my lord,
The Lady Constance in a frenzy died
Three days before.  But this from rumour's tongue
I idly heard; if true or false I know not.                   124

   *K. John.* Withhold thy speed, dreadful occasion!
O, make a league with me, till I have pleas'd
My discontented peers.  What! mother dead!
How wildly then walks my estate in France!                   128

---

106 fearful: *full of fear*         109 weather: *tempest*
111 preparation: *expedition*   113 copy: *pattern*   115 arriv'd: *landed*
116 intelligence: *obtaining of secret information*
118 drawn: *assembled*       119-123 My liege . . . before; *cf. n.*
124 idly: *carelessly*  125 occasion: *course of events*  128 estate: *power*

Under whose conduct came those powers of France
That thou for truth giv'st out are landed here?
  *Mess.* Under the Dauphin.
  *K. John.*            Thou hast made me giddy
With these ill tidings.

    *Enter Bastard, and Peter of Pomfret.*

                   Now, what says the world 132
To your proceedings? do not seek to stuff
My head with more ill news, for it is full.
  *Bast.* But if you be afeard to hear the worst,
Then let the worst unheard fall on your head.    136
  *K. John.* Bear with me, cousin, for I was amaz'd
Under the tide; but now I breathe again
Aloft the flood, and can give audience
To any tongue, speak it of what it will.    140
  *Bast.* How I have sped among the clergymen,
The sums I have collected shall express.
But as I travail'd hither through the land,
I find the people strangely fantasied;    144
Possess'd with rumours, full of idle dreams,
Not knowing what they fear, but full of fear.
And here's a prophet that I brought with me
From forth the streets of Pomfret, whom I found  148
With many hundreds treading on his heels;
To whom he sung, in rude harsh-sounding rimes,
That, ere the next Ascension-day at noon,
Your highness should deliver up your crown.    152
  *K. John.* Thou idle dreamer, wherefore didst thou
    so?
  *Peter.* Foreknowing that the truth will fall out so.
  *K. John.* Hubert, away with him; imprison him;

---

129 conduct: *leadership*    137 amaz'd: *perplexed*    139 Aloft: *above*
141 sped: *fared*              144 fantasied: *possessed of fancies*
148 forth: *out*                         153 idle: *foolish*

And on that day at noon, whereon he says          156
I shall yield up my crown, let him be hang'd.
Deliver him to safety, and return,
For I must use thee.

                         [*Exit Hubert, with Peter.*]
                              O my gentle cousin,
Hear'st thou the news abroad, who are arriv'd?    160

    *Bast.* The French, my lord; men's mouths are full
    of it.
Besides, I met Lord Bigot and Lord Salisbury,
With eyes as red as new-enkindled fire,
And others more, going to seek the grave          164
Of Arthur, whom they say is kill'd to-night
On your suggestion.

    *K. John.*                  Gentle kinsman, go,
And thrust thyself into their companies.
I have a way to win their loves again;            168
Bring them before me.

    *Bast.*                   I will seek them out.

    *K. John.* Nay, but make haste; the better foot be-
    fore.
O, let me have no subject enemies,
When adverse foreigners affright my towns         172
With dreadful pomp of stout invasion.
Be Mercury, set feathers to thy heels,
And fly like thought from them to me again.

    *Bast.* The spirit of the time shall teach me speed. 176
                                        *Exit.*

    *K. John.* Spoke like a sprightful noble gentleman.
Go after him; for he perhaps shall need
Some messenger betwixt me and the peers;
And be thou he.

158 safety: *custody*                          159 gentle: *noble*
166 suggestion: *secret incitement*            167 companies: *company*
173 stout: *bold*                              177 sprightful: *spirited*

*Mess.*                With all my heart, my liege.        180

[*Exit.*]

*K. John.* My mother dead!

### Enter Hubert.

*Hub.* My lord, they say five moons were seen to-
        night;
Four fixed, and the fifth did whirl about
The other four in wondrous motion.                     184

*K. John.* Five moons!

*Hub.*                Old men and beldams in the streets
Do prophesy upon it dangerously.
Young Arthur's death is common in their mouths;
And when they talk of him, they shake their heads  188
And whisper one another in the ear;
And he that speaks, doth gripe the hearer's wrist,
Whilst he that hears makes fearful action,
With wrinkled brows, with nods, with rolling eyes.  192
I saw a smith stand with his hammer, thus,
The whilst his iron did on the anvil cool,
With open mouth swallowing a tailor's news;
Who, with his shears and measure in his hand,          196
Standing on slippers, which his nimble haste
Had falsely thrust upon contrary feet,
Told of a many thousand warlike French,
That were embattailed and rank'd in Kent.             200
Another lean unwash'd artificer
Cuts off his tale and talks of Arthur's death.

*K. John.* Why seek'st thou to possess me with these
        fears?
Why urgest thou so oft young Arthur's death?      204
Thy hand hath murder'd him.  I had a mighty cause

185 beldams: *hags*                    186 prophesy: *make predictions*
191 action: *gesticulation*                      198 contrary: *wrong*
200 embattailed: *set in order of battle*

To wish him dead, but thou hadst none to kill him.

   *Hub.* No had, my lord? why, did you not provoke
     me?

   *K. John.* It is the curse of kings to be attended 208
By slaves that take their humours for a warrant
To break within the bloody house of life,
And on the winking of authority
To understand a law, to know the meaning    212
Of dangerous majesty, when, perchance, it frowns
More upon humour than advis'd respect.

   *Hub.* Here is your hand and seal for what I did.

   *K. John.* O, when the last accompt 'twixt heaven and
     earth    216
Is to be made, then shall this hand and seal
Witness against us to damnation!
How oft the sight of means to do ill deeds
Makes deeds ill done!  Hadst not thou been by,   220
A fellow by the hand of nature mark'd,
Quoted and sign'd to do a deed of shame,
This murther had not come into my mind;
But taking note of thy abhorr'd aspect,    224
Finding thee fit for bloody villainy,
Apt, liable to be employ'd in danger,
I faintly broke with thee of Arthur's death;
And thou, to be endeared to a king,    228
Made it no conscience to destroy a prince.

   *Hub.* My lord,—

   *K. John.* Hadst thou but shook thy head or made a
     pause
When I spake darkly what I purposed,    232

207 No had: *had I not*    provoke: *incite*    209 humours: *caprices*
210 bloody: *containing blood*   211-214 *Cf. n.*   216 accompt: *account*
222 Quoted: *set down as in writing*    sign'd: *marked out*
224 abhorr'd: *abominable*    aspect: *appearance*
226 Apt: *ready*   liable: *suitable*
227 faintly: *half-heartedly*    broke with thee: *suggested the subject*
229 no conscience: *no matter of conscience*    232 darkly: *vaguely*

Or turn'd an eye of doubt upon my face,
As bid me tell my tale in express words,
Deep shame had struck me dumb, made me break
     off,
And those thy fears might have wrought fears in
     me.     236
But thou didst understand me by my signs
And didst in signs again parley with sin;
Yea, without stop, didst let thy heart consent,
And consequently thy rude hand to act     240
The deed which both our tongues held vile to name.
Out of my sight, and never see me more!
My nobles leave me; and my state is brav'd,
Even at my gates, with ranks of foreign powers.    244
Nay, in the body of this fleshly land,
This kingdom, this confine of blood and breath,
Hostility and civil tumult reigns
Between my conscience and my cousin's death.     248

    *Hub.* Arm you against your other enemies:
I'll make a peace between your soul and you.
Young Arthur is alive: this hand of mine
Is yet a maiden and an innocent hand,     252
Not painted with the crimson spots of blood.
Within this bosom never enter'd yet
The dreadful motion of a murderous thought;
And you have slander'd nature in my form,     256
Which, howsoever rude exteriorly,
Is yet the cover of a fairer mind
Than to be butcher of an innocent child.

    *K. John.* Doth Arthur live? O, haste thee to the
     peers!     260

---

234 As: *as if to*          240 consequently: *by way of consequence*
243 brav'd: *defied*
245 fleshly: *consisting of flesh*     land: *(applied to the human body)*
246 confine: *territory*             247 civil tumult: *internal war*
252 maiden: *bloodless*     255 motion: *impulse*     256 form: *image*

Throw this report on their incensed rage,
And make them tame to their obedience.
Forgive the comment that my passion made
Upon thy feature; for my rage was blind,                264
And foul imaginary eyes of blood
Presented thee more hideous than thou art.
O, answer not; but to my closet bring
The angry lords, with all expedient haste.              268
I conjure thee but slowly; run more fast.

*Exeunt.*

### Scene Three

[*The Same.  Before the Castle*]

*Enter Arthur, on the Walls.*

*Arth.* The wall is high; and yet will I leap down.
Good ground, be pitiful and hurt me not!
There's few or none do know me; if they did,
This ship-boy's semblance hath disguis'd me quite.      4
I am afraid; and yet I'll venture it.
If I get down, and do not break my limbs,
I'll find a thousand shifts to get away:
As good to die and go, as die and stay.                 8

[*Leaps down.*]

O me! my uncle's spirit is in these stones!
Heaven take my soul, and England keep my bones!

*Dies.*

*Enter Pembroke, Salisbury, and Bigot.*

*Sal.* Lords, I will meet him at Saint Edmundsbury.

262 make . . . tame: *subjugate*            263 comment: *criticism*
264 feature: *shape*                        265 imaginary: *imaginative*
267 closet: *private room*                  268 expedient: *expeditious*
269 conjure: *adjure*                       4 ship-boy's semblance; *cf. n.*
7 shifts: *contrivances*                    11 him; *cf. n.*

It is our safety, and we must embrace                          12
This gentle offer of the perilous time.

*Pem.* Who brought that letter from the cardinal?

*Sal.* The Count Melun, a noble lord of France;
Whose private with me of the Dauphin's love          16
Is much more general than these lines import.

*Big.* To-morrow morning let us meet him then.

*Sal.* Or rather then set forward; for 'twill be
Two long days' journey, lords, or e'er we meet.       20

### *Enter Bastard.*

*Bast.* Once more to-day well met, distemper'd
    lords!
The king by me requests your presence straight.

*Sal.* The king hath dispossess'd himself of us:
We will not line his thin bestained cloak                24
With our pure honours, nor attend the foot
That leaves the print of blood where'er it walks.
Return and tell him so: we know the worst.

*Bast.* Whate'er you think, good words, I think, were
    best.                                      28

*Sal.* Our griefs, and not our manners, reason now.

*Bast.* But there is little reason in your grief;
Therefore 'twere reason you had manners now.

*Pem.* Sir, sir, impatience hath his privilege.          32

*Bast.* 'Tis true: to hurt his master, no man else.

*Sal.* This is the prison.

                         *[Seeing Arthur.]*
                 What is he lies here?

*Pem.* O death, made proud with pure and princely
    beauty!
The earth had not a hole to hide this deed.               36

---

12 safety: *safeguard*    embrace: *welcome*
16 private: *private communication*    love: *friendship*
17 general: *far-reaching*    20 or e'er: *before*    21 distemper'd: *vexed*
22 straight: *immediately*    29 griefs: *grievances*    reason: *discourse*

*Sal.* Murther, as hating what himself hath done,
Doth lay it open to urge on revenge.

    *Big.* Or when he doom'd this beauty to a grave,
Found it too precious princely for a grave.    40

    *Sal.* Sir Richard, what think you? You have be-
       held.
Or have you read or heard? or could you think?
Or do you almost think, although you see,
That you do see? could thought, without this ob-
    ject,    44
Form such another? This is the very top,
The height, the crest, or crest unto the crest,
Of murther's arms; this is the bloodiest shame,
The wildest savagery, the vilest stroke,    48
That ever wall-eyed wrath or staring rage
Presented to the tears of soft remorse.

    *Pem.* All murthers past do stand excus'd in this:
And this, so sole and so unmatchable,    52
Shall give a holiness, a purity,
To the yet unbegotten sin of times;
And prove a deadly bloodshed but a jest,
Exampled by this heinous spectacle.    56

    *Bast.* It is a damned and a bloody work;
The graceless action of a heavy hand,
If that it be the work of any hand.

    *Sal.* If that it be the work of any hand!    60
We had a kind of light what would ensue.
It is the shameful work of Hubert's hand,
The practice and the purpose of the king,
From whose obedience I forbid my soul,    64
Kneeling before this ruin of sweet life,

49 wall-eyed: *glaring*    rage: *madness*    50 remorse: *tenderness*
52 sole: *unique*                                54 times: *future times*
55 bloodshed: *act of bloodshed*    56 Exampled: *furnished a precedent*
58 graceless: *unchristian*    heavy: *wicked*
63 practice: *siratagem*

And breathing to his breathless excellence
The incense of a vow, a holy vow,
Never to taste the pleasures of the world,                68
Never to be infected with delight,
Nor conversant with ease and idleness,
Till I have set a glory to this hand,
By giving it the worship of revenge.                72

*Pem.* ⎫
*Big.* ⎭ Our souls religiously confirm thy words.

### *Enter Hubert.*

*Hub.* Lords, I am hot with haste in seeking you:
Arthur doth live; the king hath sent for you.
*Sal.* O! he is bold and blushes not at death.                76
Avaunt, thou hateful villain! get thee gone!
*Hub.* I am no villain.
*Sal.* [*Drawing his sword.*] Must I rob the law?
*Bast.* Your sword is bright, sir; put it up again.
*Sal.* Not till I sheathe it in a murtherer's skin.                80
*Hub.* Stand back, Lord Salisbury, stand back, I
        say!
By heaven, I think my sword's as sharp as yours.
I would not have you, lord, forget yourself,
Nor tempt the danger of my true defence;                84
Lest I, by marking of your rage, forget
Your worth, your greatness, and nobility.
*Big.* Out, dunghill! dar'st thou brave a nobleman?
*Hub.* Not for my life; but yet I dare defend                88
My innocent life against an emperor.
*Sal.* Thou art a murtherer.
*Hub.*                         Do not prove me so;
Yet I am none.   Whose tongue soe'er speaks false,

69 infected: *affected*        71 this hand; *cf. n.*        72 worship: *honor*
73 religiously: *under a solemn obligation*
77 Avaunt: *begone*                                84 true: *just*

Not truly speaks; who speaks not truly, lies.      92

   *Pem.* Cut him to pieces.

   *Bast.*                                   Keep the peace, I say.

   *Sal.* Stand by, or I shall gall you, Faulconbridge.

   *Bast.* Thou wert better gall the devil, Salisbury.

If thou but frown on me, or stir thy foot,         96

Or teach thy hasty spleen to do me shame,

I'll strike thee dead.  Put up thy sword betime,

Or I'll so maul you and your toasting-iron,

That you shall think the devil is come from hell.   100

   *Big.* What wilt thou do, renowned Faulconbridge?

Second a villain and a murtherer?

   *Hub.* Lord Bigot, I am none.

   *Big.*                                   Who kill'd this prince?

   *Hub.* 'Tis not an hour since I left him well.   104

I honour'd him, I lov'd him; and will weep

My date of life out for his sweet life's loss.

   *Sal.* Trust not those cunning waters of his eyes,

For villainy is not without such rheum;            108

And he, long traded in it, makes it seem

Like rivers of remorse and innocency.

Away with me, all you whose souls abhor

Th' uncleanly savours of a slaughter-house,        112

For I am stifled with this smell of sin.

   *Big.* Away toward Bury, to the Dauphin there!

   *Pem.* There tell the king he may inquire us out.

                         *Ex[eunt] Lords.*

   *Bast.* Here's a good world!  Knew you of this fair work?      116

Beyond the infinite and boundless reach

Of mercy, if thou didst this deed of death,

---

94 Stand by: *stand aside*    gall: *make to smart*
99 toasting-iron: *toasting fork (i.e. sword)*
                                    104 *Cf. n.*
106 date: *term of existence*        109 traded: *expert*
112 savours: *smells*      116 good world: *fine state of things*

Art thou damn'd, Hubert.

    *Hub.*              Do but hear me, sir.

    *Bast.* Ha! I'll tell thee what;          120
Thou'rt damn'd as black—nay, nothing is so black;
Thou art more deep damn'd than Prince Lucifer;
There is not yet so ugly a fiend of hell
As thou shalt be, if thou didst kill this child.    124

    *Hub.* Upon my soul,—

    *Bast.*             If thou didst but consent
To this most cruel act, do but despair;
And if thou want'st a cord, the smallest thread
That ever spider twisted from her womb    128
Will serve to strangle thee; a rush will be a beam
To hang thee on.  Or wouldst thou drown thyself,
Put but a little water in a spoon,
And it shall be as all the ocean,    132
Enough to stifle such a villain up.
I do suspect thee very grievously.

    *Hub.* If I in act, consent, or sin of thought,
Be guilty of the stealing that sweet breath    136
Which was embounded in this beauteous clay,
Let hell want pains enough to torture me.
I left him well.

    *Bast.*        Go, bear him in thine arms.
I am amaz'd, methinks, and lose my way    140
Among the thorns and dangers of this world.
How easy dost thou take all England up!
From forth this morsel of dead royalty,
The life, the right and truth of all this realm    144
Is fled to heaven; and England now is left
To tug and scamble and to part by th' teeth
The unow'd interest of proud swelling state.

134 grievously: *strongly*         137 embounded: *enclosed*
146 scamble: *scramble*
147 unow'd: *unowned*    interest: *title, right*

Now for the bare-pick'd bone of majesty   148
Doth dogged war bristle his angry crest,
And snarleth in the gentle eyes of peace.
Now powers from home and discontents at home
Meet in one line; and vast confusion waits,   152
As doth a raven on a sick-fallen beast,
The imminent decay of wrested pomp.
Now happy he whose cloak and center can
Hold out this tempest. Bear away that child,   156
And follow me with speed: I'll to the king:
A thousand businesses are brief in hand,
And heaven itself doth frown upon the land.

                                      *Exit.*

## ACT FIFTH

### Scene One

*[The Same. A Room in the Palace]*

*Enter King John, and Pandulph, [with the crown, and] Attendants.*

*K. John.* Thus have I yielded up into your hand
The circle of my glory.

*Pand.* [*Giving John the crown.*] Take again
From this my hand, as holding of the pope,
Your sovereign greatness and authority.   4

*K. John.* Now keep your holy word: go meet the French,
And from his holiness use all your power
To stop their marches 'fore we are enflam'd.

149 dogged: *fierce*                  151 discontents: *mutineers*
152 vast: *extending far and wide*   154 wrested pomp: *usurped majesty*
155 center: *girdle, ceinture*
158 brief in hand: *quickly to be undertaken*        2 circle: *crown*
4 sovereign: *of supreme power or excellence*
7 'fore: *before*     enflam'd: *set on fire*

Our discontented counties do revolt;                     8
Our people quarrel with obedience,
Swearing allegiance and the love of soul
To stranger blood, to foreign royalty.
This inundation of mistemper'd humour             12
Rests by you only to be qualified:
Then pause not; for the present time's so sick,
That present med'cine must be minister'd,
Or overthrow incurable ensues.                           16

   *Pand.* It was my breath that blew this tempest up,
Upon your stubborn usage of the pope;
But since you are a gentle convertite,
My tongue shall hush again this storm of war      20
And make fair weather in your blust'ring land.
On this Ascension-day, remember well,
Upon your oath of service to the pope,
Go I to make the French lay down their arms.     24
                             *Exit.*

   *K. John.* Is this Ascension-day? Did not the prophet
Say that before Ascension-day at noon
My crown I should give off? Even so I have.
I did suppose it should be on constraint;             28
But, heaven be thank'd, it is but voluntary.

                *Enter Bastard.*

   *Bast.* All Kent hath yielded; nothing there holds out
But Dover Castle; London hath receiv'd,
Like a kind host, the Dauphin and his powers.    32

---

8 counties: *shires; or nobles*    9 quarrel with: *set themselves against*
10 love of soul: *sincere love*        11 stranger: *strange*
12 mistemper'd: *disordered*
13 Rests by: *depends upon*     qualified: *moderated*
15 minister'd: *administered*        18 Upon: *in consequence of*
19 convertite: *convert*               27 give off: *relinquish*

Your nobles will not hear you, but are gone
To offer service to your enemy;
And wild amazement hurries up and down
The little number of your doubtful friends.            36

    *K. John.* Would not my lords return to me again
After they heard young Arthur was alive?

    *Bast.* They found him dead and cast into the streets,
An empty casket, where the jewel of life                40
By some damn'd hand was robb'd and ta'en away.

    *K. John.* That villain Hubert told me he did live.

    *Bast.* So, on my soul, he did, for aught he knew.
But wherefore do you droop? why look you sad?        44
Be great in act, as you have been in thought;
Let not the world see fear and sad distrust
Govern the motion of a kingly eye.
Be stirring as the time; be fire with fire;            48
Threaten the threat'ner, and outface the brow
Of bragging horror.  So shall inferior eyes,
That borrow their behaviours from the great,
Grow great by your example and put on               52
The dauntless spirit of resolution.
Away! and glister like the god of war
When he intendeth to become the field:
Show boldness and aspiring confidence.               56
What! shall they seek the lion in his den
And fright him there? and make him tremble there?
O, let it not be said!  Forage, and run
To meet displeasure farther from the doors,           60
And grapple with him ere he come so nigh.

    *K. John.* The legate of the pope hath been with
      me,
And I have made a happy peace with him;

---

35 amazement: *distraction*        36 doubtful: *apprehensive*
49 outface: *stare down*              55 become: *adorn*
59 Forage: *range abroad for food*

And he hath promis'd to dismiss the powers     64
Led by the Dauphin.

    *Bast.*              O inglorious league!
Shall we, upon the footing of our land,
Send fair-play orders and make compromise,
Insinuation, parley and base truce     68
To arms invasive?  Shall a beardless boy,
A cocker'd silken wanton, brave our fields,
And flesh his spirit in a warlike soil,
Mocking the air with colours idly spread,     72
And find no check?  Let us, my liege, to arms!
Perchance the cardinal cannot make your peace;
Or if he do, let it at least be said
They saw we had a purpose of defence.     76

    *K. John.* Have thou the ordering of this present
    time.

    *Bast.* Away then, with good courage! yet, I know,
Our party may well meet a prouder foe.

                             *Exeunt.*

## Scene Two

*[A Plain, near St. Edmundsbury.  The French
Camp]*

*Enter (in arms) Dauphin [Lewis], Salisbury, Melun,
Pembroke, Bigot, Soldiers.*

    *Lew.* My Lord Melun, let this be copied out,
And keep it safe for our remembrance.
Return the precedent to those lords again;
That, having our fair order written down,     4

66 footing: *surface for the foot*
67 fair-play orders: *equitable conditions*        69 invasive: *invading*
70 cocker'd silken wanton: *spoilt or pampered child*
71 flesh: *initiate in bloodshed*          72 idly: *carelessly*
73 liege: *sovereign lord*                    79 *Cf. n.*
3 precedent: *original draft of document*    4 order: *arrangement*

Both they and we, perusing o'er these notes,
May know wherefore we took the sacrament,
And keep our faiths firm and inviolable.

   *Sal.* Upon our sides it never shall be broken.    **8**
And, noble Dauphin, albeit we swear
A voluntary zeal, and an unurg'd faith
To your proceedings; yet, believe me, prince,
I am not glad that such a sore of time    **12**
Should seek a plaster by contemn'd revolt,
And heal the inveterate canker of one wound
By making many. O, it grieves my soul
That I must draw this metal from my side    **16**
To be a widow-maker! O! and there
Where honourable rescue and defence
Cries out upon the name of Salisbury.
But such is the infection of the time,    **20**
That, for the health and physic of our right,
We cannot deal but with the very hand
Of stern injustice and confused wrong.
And is 't not pity, O my grieved friends,    **24**
That we, the sons and children of this isle,
Were born to see so sad an hour as this;
Wherein we step after a stranger, march
Upon her gentle bosom, and fill up    **28**
Her enemies' ranks,—I must withdraw and weep
Upon the spot of this enforced cause,—
To grace the gentry of a land remote,
And follow unacquainted colours here?    **32**
What, here? O nation! that thou couldst remove!
That Neptune's arms, who clippeth thee about,
Would bear thee from the knowledge of thyself,

---

6 took the sacrament; *cf. n.*
14 inveterate: *of long standing*    canker: *ulcer*
16 metal: *sword*    19 Cries out upon: *invokes*
22 deal: *act*    30 spot: *stain, disgrace*
32 unacquainted: *foreign*
35 knowledge: *consciousness*

13 contemn'd: *despicable*
21 physic: *cure*
enforced: *involuntary*
34 clippeth: *embraceth*

And gripple thee unto a pagan shore,                              36
Where these two Christian armies might combine
The blood of malice in a vein of league,
And not to spend it so unneighbourly!

   *Lew.* A noble temper dost thou show in this;    40
And great affections wrastling in thy bosom
Doth make an earthquake of nobility.
O! what a noble combat hast [thou] fought
Between compulsion and a brave respect!                           44
Let me wipe off this honourable dew,
That silverly doth progress on thy cheeks.
My heart hath melted at a lady's tears,
Being an ordinary inundation;                                     48
But this effusion of such manly drops,
This shower, blown up by tempest of the soul,
Startles mine eyes, and makes me more amaz'd
Than had I seen the vaulty top of heaven                          52
Figur'd quite o'er with burning meteors.
Lift up thy brow, renowned Salisbury,
And with a great heart heave away this storm;
Commend these waters to those baby eyes                           56
That never saw the giant world enrag'd,
Nor met with fortune other than at feasts,
Full warm of blood, of mirth, of gossiping.
Come, come; for thou shalt thrust thy hand as deep 60
Into the purse of rich prosperity
As Lewis himself; so, nobles, shall you all,
That knit your sinews to the strength of mine.

### *Enter Pandulph.*

36 gripple: *grapple; cf. n.*      38 a vein of league; *cf. n.*
40 temper: *condition of mind*
41 affections: *emotions*    wrastling: *wrestling*    43, 44 *Cf. n.*
45 dew: *tears*
46 silverly: *with silvery brightness*    progress: *move along*
52 had I: *if I had*    53 Figur'd: *figured as in a pattern*
56 Commend: *leave*    waters: *tears*    59 Full: *exceedingly*

And even there, methinks, an angel spake:                    64
Look, where the holy legate comes apace,
To give us warrant from the hand of heaven,
And on our actions set the name of right
With holy breath.

    *Pand.*        Hail, noble prince of France!    68
The next is this: King John hath reconcil'd
Himself to Rome; his spirit is come in
That so stood out against the holy church,
The great metropolis and see of Rome.                        72
Therefore thy threat'ning colours now wind up,
And tame the savage spirit of wild war,
That, like a lion foster'd up at hand,
It may lie gently at the foot of peace,                      76
And be no further harmful than in show.

    *Lew.* Your grace shall pardon me; I will not back.
I am too high-born to be propertied,
To be a secondary at control,                                80
Or useful serving-man and instrument
To any sovereign state throughout the world.
Your breath first kindled the dead coal of wars
Between this chastis'd kingdom and myself,                    84
And brought in matter that should feed this fire;
And now 'tis far too huge to be blown out
With that same weak wind which enkindled it.
You taught me how to know the face of right,                 88
Acquainted me with interest to this land,
Yea, thrust this enterprise into my heart;
And come ye now to tell me John hath made
His peace with Rome? What is that peace to me?   92
I, by the honour of my marriage-bed,
After young Arthur, claim this land for mine;

---

64 an angel spake; *cf. n.*        78 shall: *must*     back: *go back*
79 propertied: *treated as a property*      80 secondary: *mere agent*
85 matter: *fuel*      89 interest: *claim*      93 *Cf. n.*

And, now it is half-conquer'd, must I back
Because that John hath made his peace with Rome? 96
Am I Rome's slave? What penny hath Rome borne,
What men provided, what munition sent,
To underprop this action? Is 't not I
That undergo this charge? Who else but I,            100
And such as to my claim are liable,
Sweat in this business and maintain this war?
Have I not heard these islanders shout out,
*Vive le roy!* as I have bank'd their towns?         104
Have I not here the best cards for the game
To win this easy match play'd for a crown?
And shall I now give o'er the yielded set?
No, no, on my soul, it never shall be said.          108

    *Pand.* You look but on the outside of this work.

    *Lew.* Outside or inside, I will not return
Till my attempt so much be glorified
As to my ample hope was promised                     112
Before I drew this gallant head of war,
And cull'd these fiery spirits from the world,
To outlook conquest and to win renown
Even in the jaws of danger and of death.             116

                        *[Trumpet sounds.]*

What lusty trumpet thus doth summon us?

          *Enter Bastard.*

    *Bast.* According to the fair play of the world,
Let me have audience; I am sent to speak.
My holy Lord of Milan, from the king                 120
I come, to learn how you have dealt for him;
And, as you answer, I do know the scope
And warrant limited unto my tongue.

---

99 underprop: *maintain*     101 liable: *subject*     104 bank'd: *coasted*
106 match: *contest*     107 set: *game*     113 head: *armed force*
115 outlook: *stare down*                     117 lusty: *vigorous*
122 as: *according as*     scope: *latitude*     123 limited: *appointed*

*Pand.* The Dauphin is too wilful-opposite,                    124
And will not temporize with my entreaties:
He flatly says he'll not lay down his arms.

*Bast.* By all the blood that ever fury breath'd,
The youth says well.  Now hear our English king; 128
For thus his royalty doth speak in me.
He is prepar'd, and reason too he should.
This apish and unmannerly approach,
This harness'd masque and unadvised revel,       132
This unheard sauciness and boyish troops,
The king doth smile at; and is well prepar'd
To whip this dwarfish war, these pigmy arms,
From out the circle of his territories.           136
That hand which had the strength, even at your
          door,
To cudgel you and make you take the hatch;
To dive, like buckets, in concealed wells;
To crouch in litter of your stable planks;        140
To lie like pawns lock'd up in chests and trunks;
To hug with swine; to seek sweet safety out
In vaults and prisons; and to thrill and shake,
Even at the crying of your nation's crow,         144
Thinking this voice an armed Englishman:
Shall that victorious hand be feebled here
That in your chambers gave you chastisement?
No! Know the gallant monarch is in arms,          148
And like an eagle o'er his aiery towers,
To souse annoyance that comes near his nest.
And you degenerate, you ingrate revolts,

124 wilful-opposite: *stubbornly hostile*     125 temporize: *come to terms*
126 flatly: *absolutely*                           131 apish: *fantastic*
132 harness'd: *in armor*      unadvised: *thoughtless*
133 unheard: *unheard of*                      136 circle: *circuit*
138 take the hatch: *jump over the half-door, gate, or wicket*
141 pawns: *pledges*              144 your nation's crow; *cf. n.*
149 aiery: *brood (of an eagle)*        towers: *soars*
150 souse: *swoop down upon*      annoyance: *cause of hurt or pain*
151 ingrate revolts: *ungrateful rebels*

You bloody Neroes, ripping up the womb                          152
Of your dear mother England, blush for shame:
For your own ladies and pale-visag'd maids
Like Amazons come tripping after drums,
Their thimbles into armed gauntlets change,          156
Their neelds to lances, and their gentle hearts
To fierce and bloody inclination.

    *Lew.* There end thy brave, and turn thy face in
      peace;
We grant thou canst outscold us.   Fare thee well; 160
We hold our time too precious to be spent
With such a brabbler.

    *Pand.*           Give me leave to speak.

    *Bast.* No, I will speak.

    *Lew.*          We will attend to neither.
Strike up the drums; and let the tongue of war      164
Plead for our interest and our being here.

    *Bast.* Indeed, your drums, being beaten, will cry
      out;
And so shall you, being beaten.   Do but start
An echo with the clamour of thy drum,                 168
And even at hand a drum is ready brac'd
That shall reverberate all as loud as thine;
Sound but another, and another shall
As loud as thine rattle the welkin's ear              172
And mock the deep-mouth'd thunder.   For at hand,—
Not trusting to this halting legate here,
Whom he hath us'd rather for sport than need,—
Is warlike John; and in his forehead sits             176
A bare-ribb'd death, whose office is this day
To feast upon whole thousands of the French.

154 maids: *daughters*   157 neelds: *needles*   158 inclination: *purpose*
159 brave: *bravado*                  162 brabbler: *brawler*
164 Strike up: *beat loudly*   169 brac'd: *strung up, made tight*
172 rattle: *assail with a rattling noise*   welkin's: *sky's*
174 halting: *ineffectual*                177 office: *function*

*Lew.* Strike up our drums, to find this danger out.

*Bast.* And thou shalt find it, Dauphin, do not
doubt.

*Exeunt.*

## Scene Three

[*The Same.   A Field of Battle*]

*Alarums.   Enter* [*King*] *John and Hubert.*

*K. John.* How goes the day with us?  O, tell me,
Hubert!

*Hub.* Badly, I fear.   How fares your majesty?

*K. John.* This fever, that hath troubled me so
long,

Lies heavy on me: O, my heart is sick!          4

*Enter a Messenger.*

*Mess.* My lord, your valiant kinsman, Faulconbridge,

Desires your majesty to leave the field,

And send him word by me which way you go.

*K. John.* Tell him, toward Swinstead, to the abbey
there.                                          8

*Mess.* Be of good comfort: for the great supply

That was expected by the Dauphin here,

Are wrack'd three nights ago on Goodwin sands.

This news was brought to Richard but even now.   12

The French fight coldly, and retire themselves.

*K. John.* Ay me! this tyrant fever burns me up,

And will not let me welcome this good news.

Set on toward Swinstead: to my litter straight;   16

Weakness possesseth me, and I am faint.

*Exeunt.*

8 Swinstead; *cf. n.*
9 supply: *reinforcements*                    11 wrack'd: *shipwrecked*
13 coldly: *without heat or passion*          14 tyrant: *pitiless*

## Scene Four

*[The Same.   Another Part of the Same]*

*Enter Salisbury, Pembroke, and Bigot [and Others].*

*Sal.* I did not think the king so stor'd with friends.

*Pem.* Up once again; put spirit in the French:
If they miscarry we miscarry too.

*Sal.* That misbegotten devil, Faulconbridge,          4
In spite of spite, alone upholds the day.

*Pem.* They say King John, sore sick, hath left the
field.

*Enter Melun wounded [and led by Soldiers].*

*Mel.* Lead me to the revolts of England here.

*Sal.* When we were happy we had other names.        8

*Pem.* It is the Count Melun.

*Sal.*                              Wounded to death.

*Mel.* Fly, noble English; you are bought and sold;
Unthread the rude eye of rebellion,
And welcome home again discarded faith.              12
Seek out King John and fall before his feet;
For if the French be lords of this loud day,
He means to recompense the pains you take
By cutting off your heads.   Thus hath he sworn,     16
And I with him, and many moe with me,
Upon the altar at Saint Edmundsbury;
Even on that altar where we swore to you
Dear amity and everlasting love.                     20

*Sal.* May this be possible? may this be true?

*Mel.* Have I not hideous death within my view,
Retaining but a quantity of life,

---

1 stor'd: *provided*                             3 miscarry: *come to grief*
5 In spite of spite: *notwithstanding anything*         6 sore: *grievously*
11 Unthread the rude eye: *retrace the rough path*
12 home: *to its right or proper place*               15 He: *i.e. the Dauphin*
17 moe: *more*                                        23 quantity: *fragment*

Which bleeds away, even as a form of wax                    24
Resolveth from his figure 'gainst the fire?
What in the world should make me now deceive,
Since I must lose the use of all deceit?
Why should I then be false, since it is true             28
That I must die here and live hence by truth?
I say again, if Lewis do win the day,
He is forsworn, if e'er those eyes of yours
Behold another day break in the east.                    32
But even this night, whose black contagious **breath**
Already smokes about the burning crest
Of the old, feeble, and day-wearied sun,
Even this ill night, your breathing shall expire,        36
Paying the fine of rated treachery
Even with a treacherous fine of all your lives,
If Lewis by your assistance win the day.
Commend me to one Hubert with your king;                 40
The love of him, and this respect besides,
For that my grandsire was an Englishman,
Awakes my conscience to confess all this.
In lieu whereof, I pray you, bear me hence               44
From forth the noise and rumour of the field,
Where I may think the remnant of my thoughts
In peace, and part this body and my soul
With contemplation and devout desires.                   48

    *Sal.* We do believe thee, and beshrew my soul
But I do love the favour and the form
Of this most fair occasion, by the which
We will untread the steps of damned flight,              52

24 a form of wax; *cf. n.*    25 Resolveth: *dissolveth*    figure: *shape*
33 contagious: *pestilential*   36 breathing: *life*   37 rated: *appraised*
38 fine: *end*    41 respect: *consideration*    42 For that: *because*
44 In lieu whereof: *in return for which*
45 From forth: *away from*    rumour: *confused noise*
47 part: *undergo the parting of*       49 beshrew: *a curse upon*
50 But: *if . . . not*    favour: *appearance*    form: *outward aspect*
52 untread: *retrace*

And like a bated and retired flood,
Leaving our rankness and irregular course,
Stoop low within those bounds we have o'erlook'd,
And calmly run on in obedience,                    56
Even to our ocean, to our great King John.
My arm shall give thee help to bear thee hence,
For I do see the cruel pangs of death
Right in thine eye. Away, my friends! New flight; 60
And happy newness, that intends old right.

                    *Exeunt [leading off Melun].*


## Scene Five

### [*The Same.  The French Camp*]

*Enter Dauphin [Lewis], and his Train.*

*Lew.* The sun of heaven methought was loath to
    set,
But stay'd and made the western welkin blush,
When English measure backward their own ground
In faint retire.  O, bravely came we off,            4
When with a volley of our needless shot,
After such bloody toil, we bid good night;
And wound our tott'ring colours clearly up,
Last in the field, and almost lords of it!           8

*Enter a Messenger.*

*Mess.* Where is my prince, the Dauphin?
*Lew.*                    Here: what news?
*Mess.* The Count Melun is slain; the English lords,

53 bated: *abated*     retired: *subsided*
54 Leaving: *giving up*     rankness: *fulness to overflowing*
55 o'erlook'd: *despised*               1 methought: *it seemed to me*
3 English: *Englishmen*     measure: *traverse*
4 faint: *timid*     retire: *retreat*     bravely: *excellently*
7 tott'ring: *in rags; or swinging in the air*     clearly: *stainlessly*

By his persuasion, are again fall'n off;
And your supply, which you have wish'd so long,     12
Are cast away and sunk, on Goodwin sands.

    *Lew.* Ah, foul, shrewd news! Beshrew thy very
      heart!
I did not think to be so sad to-night
As this hath made me. Who was he that said     16
King John did fly an hour or two before
The stumbling night did part our weary powers?

    *Mess.* Whoever spoke it, it is true, my lord.

    *Lew.* Well; keep good quarter and good care to-
      night.                                             20
The day shall not be up so soon as I,
To try the fair adventure of to-morrow.

                           *Exeunt.*


### Scene Six

*[An open Place in the neighbourhood of Swinstead
Abbey]*

*Enter Bastard and Hubert, severally.*

    *Hub.* Who's there? speak, ho! speak quickly, **or I**
      shoot.

    *Bast.* A friend. What art thou?

    *Hub.*                    Of the part of England.

    *Bast.* Whither dost thou go?

    *Hub.* What's that to thee? Why may not I de-
      mand                                               4
Of thine affairs as well as thou of mine?

    *Bast.* Hubert, I think?

    *Hub.*            Thou hast a perfect thought.

11 are . . . fall'n off: *have been faithless*    12 supply: *reinforcements*
13 cast away: *wrecked*                14 shrewd: *grievous*
18 stumbling: *causing to stumble*     20 quarter: *watch*
22 adventure: *chance*     2 part: *side*    6 perfect: *correct*

I will upon all hazards well believe
Thou art my friend, that know'st my tongue so well. ซ
Who art thou?

*Bast.*          Who thou wilt; and if thou please,
Thou mayst befriend me so much as to think
I come one way of the Plantagenets.

*Hub.* Unkind remembrance! thou and endless
          night                                                    12
Have done me shame.   Brave soldier, pardon me,
That any accent breaking from thy tongue
Should scape the true acquaintance of mine ear.

*Bast.* Come, come; sans compliment!   What news
          abroad?                                                  16

*Hub.* Why, here walk I in the black brow of night,
To find you out.

*Bast.*          Brief, then; and what's the news?

*Hub.* O! my sweet sir, news fitting to the night,
Black, fearful, comfortless, and horrible.              2ซ

*Bast.* Show me the very wound of this ill news;
I am no woman; I'll not swound at it.

*Hub.* The king, I fear, is poison'd by a monk.
I left him almost speechless; and broke out            24
To acquaint you with this evil, that you might
The better arm you to the sudden time
Than if you had at leisure known of this.

*Bast.* How did he take it? who did taste to him? 28

*Hub.* A monk, I tell you; a resolved villain,
Whose bowels suddenly burst out.   The king
Yet speaks, and peradventure may recover.

*Bast.* Whom didst thou leave to tend his majesty? 32

7 hazards: *perils*     12 *Cf. n.*     endless: *infinite*     14 accent: *word*
16 sans: *without*     18 Brief: *briefly*     19 fitting to: *harmonizing with*
24 broke out: *rushed out*                     26 sudden time: *emergency*
27 at leisure: *after delay*                    28 taste: *act as taster*
29 resolved: *resolute*

*Hub.* Why, know you not?   The lords are all come back,
And brought Prince Henry in their company;
At whose request the king hath pardon'd them,
And they are all about his majesty.                          36
    *Bast.* Withhold thine indignation, mighty heaven,
And tempt us not to bear above our power!
I'll tell thee, Hubert, half my power this night,
Passing these flats, are taken by the tide;                  40
These Lincoln Washes have devoured them;
Myself, well mounted, hardly have escap'd.
Away before! conduct me to the king;
I doubt he will be dead or ere I come.                       44
                                                    *Exeunt.*


Scene Seven

[*The Orchard in Swinstead Abbey*]

*Enter Prince Henry, Salisbury, and Bigot.*

*P. Hen.* It is too late; the life of all his blood
Is touch'd corruptibly; and his pure brain,—
Which some suppose the soul's frail dwelling-house,—
Doth, by the idle comments that it makes,                    4
Foretell the ending of mortality.

*Enter Pembroke.*

*Pem.* His highness yet doth speak, and holds belief
That, being brought into the open air,
It would allay the burning quality                           8
Of that fell poison which assaileth him.
    *P. Hen.* Let him be brought into the orchard here.

38 tempt: *put to the test*
2 corruptibly: *so as to be corrupt*          pure: *clear*
4 idle: *foolish*
6 yet: *still*                                    5 mortality: *human life*
                                                    9 fell: *fierce*

Doth he still rage?

*[Exit Bigot.]*

   *Pem.*          He is more patient
Than when you left him; even now he sung.          12
   *P. Hen.* O, vanity of sickness! fierce extremes
In their continuance will not feel themselves.
Death, having prey'd upon the outward parts,
Leaves them invisible; and his siege is now          16
Against the mind, the which he pricks and wounds
With many legions of strange fantasies,
Which, in their throng and press to that last hold,
Confound themselves. 'Tis strange that death should
      sing.          20
I am the cygnet to this pale faint swan,
Who chants a doleful hymn to his own death,
And from the organ-pipe of frailty sings
His soul and body to their lasting rest.          24
   *Sal.* Be of good comfort, prince; for you are born
To set a form upon that indigest
Which he hath left so shapeless and so rude.

   *[King] John brought in.*

   *K. John.* Ay, marry, now my soul hath elbow-
      room;          28
It would not out at windows, nor at doors.
There is so hot a summer in my bosom
That all my bowels crumble up to dust.
I am a scribbled form, drawn with a pen          32
Upon a parchment, and against this fire
Do I shrink up.
   *P. Hen.*          How fares your majesty?
   *K. John.* Poison'd, ill fare; dead, forsook, cast off;

---

11 rage: *rave*                          13 extremes: *extremities*
18 fantasies: *fanciful images*                19 hold: *stronghold*
20 Confound themselves: *mingle indistinguishably*     21, 22 Cf. *n.*
23 organ-pipe: *organ*                    26 indigest: *shapeless mass*
32 form: *portrait*                       35 ill fare: *evil lot; cf. n.*

And none of you will bid the winter come            36
To thrust his icy fingers in my maw;
Nor let my kingdom's rivers take their course
Through my burn'd bosom; nor entreat the north
To make his bleak winds kiss my parched lips       40
And comfort me with cold.  I do not ask you much:
I beg cold comfort; and you are so strait
And so ingrateful you deny me that.

    *P. Hen.*  O! that there were some virtue in my
        tears,                                         44
That might relieve you.

    *K. John.*         The salt in them is hot.
Within me is a hell; and there the poison
Is as a fiend confin'd to tyrannize
On unreprievable condemned blood.                   48

*Enter Bastard.*

    *Bast.*  O, I am scalded with my violent motion
And spleen of speed to see your majesty.

    *K. John.*  O cousin, thou art come to set mine eye!
The tackle of my heart is crack'd and burnt,        52
And all the shrouds wherewith my life should sail
Are turned to one thread, one little hair;
My heart hath one poor string to stay it by,
Which holds but till thy news be uttered;           56
And then all this thou seest is but a clod
And module of confounded royalty.

    *Bast.*  The Dauphin is preparing hitherward,
Where heaven he knows how we shall answer him:      60
For in a night the best part of my power,
As I upon advantage did remove,

---

37 maw: *stomach*   42 strait: *niggardly*   44 virtue: *healing power*
48 unreprievable: *without possibility of a reprieve*
50 spleen: *eagerness*   51 set: *close*   53 shrouds: *sail-ropes*
58 module: *counterfeit*   confounded: *ruined*
60 heaven he knows; *cf. n.*   62 advantage: *favorable opportunity*

Were in the Washes all unwarily
Devoured by the unexpected flood.          64

[*The King dies.*]

*Sal.* You breathe these dead news in as dead an
ear.
My liege! my lord! But now a king, now thus!
*P. Hen.* Even so must I run on, and even so stop.
What surety of the world, what hope, what stay,   68
When this was now a king, and now is clay?
*Bast.* Art thou gone so? I do but stay behind
To do the office for thee of revenge,
And then my soul shall wait on thee to heaven,    72
As it on earth hath been thy servant still.
Now, now, you stars, that move in your right spheres,
Where be your powers? Show now your mended
faiths,
And instantly return with me again,               76
To push destruction and perpetual shame
Out of the weak door of our fainting land.
Straight let us seek, or straight we shall be sought:
The Dauphin rages at our very heels.              80
*Sal.* It seems you know not, then, so much as we.
The Cardinal Pandulph is within at rest,
Who half an hour since came from the Dauphin,
And brings from him such offers of our peace       84
As we with honour and respect may take,
With purpose presently to leave this war.
*Bast.* He will the rather do it when he sees
Ourselves well sinewed to our defence.             88
*Sal.* Nay, 'tis in a manner done already;
For many carriages he hath dispatch'd

63 unwarily: *unexpectedly*            64 flood: *flowing in of the tide*
65 dead news: *news of death*     68 surety: *certainty*      stay: *prop*
73 still: *always*                               74 you stars; *cf. n.*
75 mended faiths: *restored loyalty*     85 respect: *self-respect*
88 sinewed: *strengthened*                  90 carriages: *vehicles*

To the sea-side, and put his cause and quarrel
To the disposing of the cardinal:        92
With whom yourself, myself, and other lords,
If you think meet, this afternoon will post
To consummate this business happily.

*Bast.* Let it be so.  And you, my noble prince,    96
With other princes that may best be spar'd,
Shall wait upon your father's funeral.

*P. Hen.* At Worcester must his body be interr'd,
For so he will'd it.

*Bast.*                Thither shall it then.        100
And happily may your sweet self put on
The lineal state and glory of the land!
To whom, with all submission, on my knee,
I do bequeath my faithful services        104
And true subjection everlastingly.

*Sal.* And the like tender of our love we make,
To rest without a spot for evermore.

*P. Hen.* I have a kind soul that would give [you]
      thanks,        108
And knows not how to do it but with tears.

*Bast.* O, let us pay the time but needful woe,
Since it hath been beforehand with our griefs.
This England never did, nor never shall,        112
Lie at the proud foot of a conqueror,
But when it first did help to wound itself.
Now these her princes are come home again,
Come the three corners of the world in arms,        116
And we shall shock them.  Nought shall make us rue,
If England to itself do rest but true.

                                  *Exeunt.*

91 put: *submitted*      92 disposing: *direction*      104 bequeath: *bestow*
110, 111 *Cf. n.*                        117 shock: *meet force with force*

# NOTES

*The Life and Death of King John.* This title is misleading. The action of the play begins in King John's thirty-fourth year and includes events during a period of about seventeen years.

I. i. S. d. *the Chatillion of France.* It is unlikely that this individual was a historical character, although he appears in *The Troublesome Raigne.* This reading, of the First Folio, seems to indicate that a title is meant, such as 'Chatelain,' or the name of a lord.

I. i. 10. *this fair island.* In Holinshed's version King Philip of France lays no claim to the throne of England, but demands, in behalf of Arthur, the French possessions of the English kings. Arthur's right to Brittany was based on that of his father, Geoffrey Plantagenet, John's elder brother. Arthur, as Duke of Brittany, was subject to Philip Augustus, who received homage from him for Normandy, Maine, Anjou, Touraine, and Poitou. Philip, in turn, supported Arthur's claim to the English crown. Thus Philip, at the opening of the play, interferes for Arthur.

I. i. 13. *Which sways usurpingly these several titles.* In history John's legal right to the crown was not questioned in England until towards the end of his reign.

I. i. 26. *cannon.* Cannon were unknown in the time of King John. Similar anachronisms occur elsewhere in this play. Cf. II. i. 37, 210, 461, 462.

I. i. 48, 49. *Our abbeys and our priories shall pay This expedition's charge.* King John, as shown elsewhere in the play, is hostile to the clergy. This attitude is a survival from *The Troublesome Raigne,* in which it is an important issue.

I. i. 49. *expedition's.* The reading of the First Folio is *expeditious.* This has generally been regarded as a misprint, and the spelling of the Second Folio has been adopted.

I. i. 54. *Cordelion.* The reading of the First Folio. Folio spelling of 'Cœur de Lion,' the nickname of King Richard I.

I. i. 94. *A half-fac'd groat.* The Bastard plays derisively on the phrase. He compares his brother's thin face to the profile on the coin, and, at the same time, uses the contemptuous Elizabethan epithet for thin-faced men. (Cf. 'This same half-faced fellow, Shadow.' *Henry IV, Part II,* III. ii. 286.) The mention in *King John* of this coin, the groat, is an anachronism.

I. i. 134-137. If Faulconbridge were the son of Richard Cœur-de-Lion, he would have rank but not the land.

I. i. 139. *Sir Robert's his, like him.* A double genitive. The Bastard means: 'If I had my brother's shape, that is, Sir Robert's,—as he has.'

I. i. 142, 143. *That in mine ear I durst not stick a rose Lest men should say, 'Look, where three-farthings goes!'* Queen Elizabeth coined in 1561 three-half-pence and three-farthing pieces of silver. The latter bore the queen's profile, with a rose behind the ear. Such silver coins were very thin, which is the point of the Bastard's taunt.

I. i. 147. *Sir Nob.* Perhaps an early use of the cant word, *Nob,* for 'head'; or a nickname for 'Robert.'

I. i. 161. *Kneel thou down Philip, but rise more great.* The First Folio reading, *rise,* which has been restored, creates a difficulty in the metre. This is removed by Steevens's reading *arise* or Pope's *rise up.*

I. i. 171. *In at the window, or else o'er the hatch.* The Bastard's comparison is to surreptitious ways of entering a house. Cf. V. ii. 138.

I. i. 173. *And have is have, however men do catch.* The substance of the proverbs quoted by the Bastard is that after attaining an object the means of attainment is of little consequence.

I. i. 177. *A landless knight makes thee a landed squire.* The Bastard, in achieving knighthood, has yielded claim to his brother's land.

I. i. 185. *'Good den, Sir Richard!'—'God-a-mercy, fellow!'—*. In this line the Bastard begins to enact an imaginary conversation.

I. i. 189, 190. *Now your traveller, He and his toothpick at my worship's mess.* The pronoun *your* is used in a general sense, 'a traveller.' The Bastard, in acting out these imaginary scenes, is ridiculing the foreign affectation, as it was then considered, of using toothpicks. He fancies himself, now a knight, addressed as 'your worship,' and in his proper place at a 'mess,' or dinner-party of four. In the succeeding lines he makes fun of courtly conversation.

I. i. 209-215. *And so am I, whether I smack or no; And not alone in habit and device, Exterior form, outward accoutrement, But from the inward motion to deliver Sweet, sweet, sweet poison for the age's tooth, Which, though I will not practise to deceive, Yet, to avoid deceit, I mean to learn.* Faulconbridge declares that he, too, is *a bastard to the time,* that is, not a true son of the age. This is so, he says, in respect to his personal appearance and also in the absence in him of the impulse to practise flattery, though to avoid being deceived he means to learn this art.

I. i. 216. *For it shall strew the footsteps of my rising.* 'As flowers are strewn in the path of the great, so will this deceit make my way to success more easy and more pleasant.'

I. i. 219. *That will take pains to blow a horn before her?* A play on the word *horn* as the symbol of the deluded husband. (Cf. II. i. 292.) For some other instances in *King John* of the frequent plays on words, cf. II. i. 323. 447, 499, 500, 590; III. i. 180, 185-

190, 211-216, 217, 218, 268-276, 279-287; and V. vii. 34, 35.

I. i. 225. *Colbrand the giant.* The Bastard alludes sarcastically to his brother's physical appearance. Colbrand, the Danish giant, was defeated by Guy of Warwick in the presence of King Athelstan. (Cf. *Henry VIII*, V. iv. 23: 'I am not Samson, nor Sir Guy, nor Colbrand.') Michael Drayton describes the combat in his *Polyolbion* (1613, 1622), 'Twelfth Song,' ll. 216-235.

I. i. 231. *Philip! sparrow!* From his chirp the sparrow was sometimes called Phip or Philip. Skelton's satirical poem, *Philip Sparrow*, had helped to popularize the phrase. The new-made knight objects jestingly to being called by his old, trivial name. He is now Sir Richard.

I. i. 237. *Could he get me? Sir Robert could not do it.* The First Folio reads: *Could get me sir Robert could not doe it.* Modern texts inserted the pronoun *he* and the interrogation point.

I. i. 244. *Knight, knight, good mother, Basilisco-like.* Theobald indicated the allusion here to the old play of *Soliman and Perseda,* supposedly by Kyd:

'*Bas.* O, I swear, I swear . . .
I, the aforesaid Basilisco——Knight, good fellow, knight, knight.
*Piston.* Knave, good fellow, knave, knave.'

In the same fashion Shakespeare makes the Bastard insist humorously on his title of knight.

I. i. 261. *Some sins do bear their privilege on earth.* 'There are *sins* that whatever be determined of them above, are not much censured *on* earth' (Johnson).

I. i. 267. *Nor keep his princely heart from Richard's hand.* Probably an allusion to the old metrical romance of *Richard Cœur-de-Lion.* Having killed with a blow of his fist the son of the Duke of Austria,

Richard was given over to the fury of a lion. Un-
daunted, he tore out the lion's heart.

*Act Second.* This scene in the Folios is called I. ii.
Lines 1-74 of the following scene (III. i.) form Act
II, and III. i. 75-end is III. i. In Act III, in the
Folios, the second and third scenes make one scene
(III. ii.). Thus III. iv. in modern texts is in the
Folios III. iii. In the last two acts the scene-division
of the Folios is identical with that of later editions.
All editions after Rowe's adhere to the modern ar-
rangement.

*Scene One.* '. . . In spite of the fact that in the
opening scene of the play Arthur's claim is represented
as a just one and John as a usurper, the present scene
by no means enlists sympathy on behalf of Arthur's
supporters. The very words in which Philip introduces Austria as the cause of the early death of Richard
Cordelion, are as a warning to the audience not to find
their heroes here' (Moore-Smith).

II. i. 1. *Lewis.* The Folio readings here and at
line 18 have been restored. Many editors have substi-
tuted *King Philip* because of the seeming appropriate-
ness of these speeches to his rôle and character in the
play. A similar change has been made in this scene
at line 150.

II. i. 2. *forerunner of thy blood.* Richard was
Arthur's uncle, being the brother of his father, Geoffrey.

II. i. 5. *By this brave duke came early to his grave.*
The old play, *The Troublesome Raigne,* caused this
historical inaccuracy. Shakespeare has confused two
enemies of Cœur-de-Lion: Austria and Vidomar, Viscount of Limoges. Richard was thrown into prison by
the Duke of Austria (1192-1193), but was mortally
wounded (1199) by an arrow before Vidomar's castle
of Chaluz.

II. i. 40. *To cull the plots of best advantages.* 'To select the stratagems that will be most to our advantage.'

II. i. 63. *An Ate.* The allusion is to the goddess of revenge or mischief. (Cf. *Julius Cæsar*, III. i. 271: 'With Ate by his side come hot from hell.')

II. i. 64, 65. *her niece, the Lady Blanch of Spain; With them a bastard of the king's deceas'd.* The word *niece* is used here as 'granddaughter.' Blanch was the daughter of Alphonso of Castile and Eleanor, the sister of King John, and the daughter of 'the mother-queen.' Line 65 is one of the few taken directly from *The Troublesome Raigne:* 'Next to them a Bastard of the King's deceast.'

II. i. 101-103. *This little abstract doth contain that large Which died in Geoffrey, and the hand of time Shall draw this brief into as huge a volume.* At line 99 King Philip points to Arthur, calling King John's attention to the boy's resemblance to Geoffrey. He now compares Geoffrey to a book and Arthur to an abstract of it. His metaphor likens Time to a writer who will gradually expand the abstract into a volume as large as the original.

II. i. 113, 114. *In any breast of strong authority, To look into the blots and stains of right.* The reading in the First Folio for *breast* is *beast*. The passage means: 'In the breast of anyone possessing the authority to examine the blots and stains which deface or injure justice.'

II. i. 119. *Excuse.* A noun, as in the First Folio, where there is no pause after the words. Most modern editors have added a mark of punctuation after *excuse*, rendering it a verb with the sense of 'pardon me.'

II. i. 123. *That thou mayst be a queen.* A similar motive is ascribed to Constance in *The Troublesome Raigne.* Holinshed, likewise, says: Elinor 'saw, if he [Arthur] were king, how his mother Constance would looke to beare most rule within the realme of England, till hir sonne should come to lawfull age, to gouerne of himselfe.'

**II. i. 127.** *Than thou and John in manners; being as like.* Constance goes on to say how Elinor and John are alike. Some texts place a comma after *John* and omit punctuation after *manners*.

**II. i. 131.** *It cannot be and if thou wert his mother.* Constance sneers at Elinor's infidelity to her husband, Louis VII, from whom she was divorced. She later married King Henry II.

**II. i. 137.** *the proverb.* The proverb alluded to is, 'Mortuo leoni et lepores insultant.' (Erasmus, *Adagia.*) 'A dead lion even hares insult.'

**II. i. 141, 142.** *O well did he become that lion's robe, That did disrobe the lion of that robe!* In *The Troublesome Raigne* Blanch says:

'Ah joy betide his soule, to whom that spoile belong'd:
  Ah Richard, how thy glorie here is wrong'd.'

**II. i. 144.** *Alcides' shoes.* The Bastard thinks the sight of a lion's skin on Austria as ridiculous as that of Hercules' (*Alcides'*) shoes on the feet of an ass. The 'shoes of Hercules' appears frequently in the old comedies: '—— Too draw the Lyons skin vpon Aesops Asse, or Hercules shoes on a childes feete . . .' (Gosson, *The School of Abuse*, 1579). Theobald offered, instead of *shoes, shows,* a noun, meaning the lion's skin worn by Hercules.

**II. i. 149.** *King Lewis.* No very satisfactory reason can be given for Austria's reference to Lewis as *King.* The most plausible emendations of this reading of the First Folio are *King,—Lewis,* which makes Austria address both King Philip and the Dauphin; or the substitution of *Philip* for *Lewis.* Of this passage Moore-Smith writes: 'If this is what Shakespeare wrote, it was a strange slip to call the king of France here *Lewis* and not *Philip.* Many editors read "King

Philip," but unfortunately the metre is against this change. While *Lewis* is generally a monosyllable in Shakespeare, *Philip* is never so.'

II. i. 150. *Lewis.* Cf. note on II. i. 1.

II. i. 156. *Britaine.* Brittany or Bretagne.

II. i. 165. *I am not worth this coil that's made for me.* A similar revelation of Arthur's character occurs in *The Troublesome Raigne:*

'Sweet Mother, cease these hastie madding fits;
For my sake let my Grandame haue her will.
O would she with her hands pull forth my heart,
I could affoord it to appease these broyles.'

II. i. 177. *eldest.* Later readings have *eld'st* to make regular the metre in the latter half of this line.

II. i. 180. *The canon of the law.* The Mosaic law (*Exodus* 20. 5): 'visiting the iniquity of the fathers upon the children unto the third and fourth generation . . .'

II. i. 185-190. *But God hath made her sin and her the plague On this removed issue, plagu'd for her, And with her plague; her sin his injury; Her injury the beadle to her sin, All punish'd in the person of this child, And all for her, a plague upon her.* In the First Folio this passage reads:

*But God hath made her sinne and her, the plague
On this remoued issue, plagued for her,
And with her plague her sinne: his iniury
Her iniurie the Beadle to her sinne,
All punish'd in the person of this childe,
And all for her, a plague vpon her.*

The punctuation adopted for line 187 is that of Roby. There follows his explanation of the passage through line 189: 'God hath made her sin and herself to be a plague to this distant child, who is punished for her and with the punishment belonging to her: God has made her sin to be an injury to Arthur, and her injurious deeds to be the executioner to punish her sin; all which (viz., her first sin and her now injurious deeds) are punished in the person of this child.' Line 190 means: 'And all for her punishment, to be a curse upon her.'

II. i. 192. *A will.* Elinor means a 'testament' made by Richard, leaving the kingdom to John. A statement to this effect occurs in Holinshed. Constance, in reply, quibbles on the word *will.* (Cf. *The Troublesome Raigne:*

'*Q. El.* I can inferre a Will
That barres the way he vrgeth by discent.
   *Const.* A Will indeede, a crabbed Womans will.')

II. i. 215. *Confronts.* The First Folio has *Comforts.* Editors who support this reading say that King John uses the word ironically.

II. i. 247. *owe.* This word is used in its modern sense; *owes* in the next line has the meaning common in Shakespeare of 'owns.'

II. i. 282. *We for the worthiest hold the right from both.* 'We keep from both sides the right which shall be reserved for that side which proves itself the most worthy.'

II. i. 292. *ox head.* A reference to horns, as a sign of the deceived husband.

II. i. 323. *Dy'd in the dying slaughter of their foes.* A play on the words, and an allusion to the savage custom of hunters dipping their hands in the blood of the slain animals.

II. i. 325. *Cit.* In this line and in lines 363, 416, 423, 480, the Folio indicates the speaker as *Hubert,* an error explainable on the supposition that the same actor took the two parts of Hubert and the citizen. At line 368 the Folio wrongly assigns the citizen's speech to *Fra*[nce], i.e. King Philip.

II. i. 352. *O now doth Death line his dead chaps with steel!* In this and in the two subsequent lines Death is conceived of as a skeleton. (Cf. III. iv. 29-35, 40.)

II. i. 357. *Cry 'havoc!' kings.* 'Command slaughter to proceed' (Johnson). (Cf. *Julius Caesar*, III. i. 273: 'Cry, "Havoc!" and let slip the dogs of war.')

II. i. 371. *Kings of our fear.* '. . . We shall trust to our strong barred gates as the protectors, or *Kings*, of our fear' (Staunton). Possibly the phrase means merely that the citizens have their fears under control. Many editors read 'Kings of ourselves.'

II. i. 378. *mutines.* An allusion to the tale of John of Giscala and Simon bar Gioras, who gave up the war between themselves to unite against the Romans. The story occurs in Josephus, *Jewish War*, V. 6 §4. Malone thinks that Shakespeare might have known the version of this episode in *A Compendious and Most Marvellous History of the Latter Times of the Jewes Common-Weale*, . . . written in Hebrew by Joseph Ben Gorion, and translated into English by Peter Morwyng, in 1575.

II. i. 425. *Dauphin.* Regularly spelled 'Dolphin' (occasionally 'Daulphin') in the Folio.

II. i. 447. *match.* A play on the word 'marriage' and the 'match' which sets off a cannon.

II. i. 477-479. *Lest zeal, now melted by the windy breath Of soft petitions, pity and remorse, Cool and congeal again to what it was.* Elinor compares zeal (i.e. King Philip's zeal in Arthur's cause) to ice which has temporarily been thawed by warm winds, but which, after they pass, will again freeze. (Cf. *The Two Gentlemen of Verona*, III. ii. 6-10.)

II. i. 509. *so vile a lout.* In history the marriage of Lewis and Blanch was fortunate. This speech is probably an echo from *The Troublesome Raigne*, in which the Bastard himself was promised the hand of Blanch. There is a pun in lines 504-508 on the legal penalty for treason, which was hanging, drawing, and quartering.

II. i. 513. *I can with ease translate it to my will.* 'I can easily bring myself to desire it.'

II. i. 527, 528. *Then do I give Volquessen, Touraine, Maine, Poitiers, and Anjou, these five provinces.* These lines are almost identical with two lines in *The Troublesome Raigne.* Volquessen was 'the ancient country of the Velocasses, whose capital was Rouen: divided in modern times into Vexin Normand and Vexin Français' (Wright).

II. i. 571-574. *Who, having no external thing to lose But the word 'maid,' cheats the poor maid of that, That smooth-fac'd gentleman, tickling Commodity, Commodity, the bias of the world. Who* refers to maids, but at the word *cheats* the construction suddenly changes, making *Commodity,* in the next line, the subject of the figure of speech. In this the *world* is compared to the *bowl* in the game of bowls. Within the *bowl* is lead, which makes it turn, when rolled, towards this heavier side. The word *bias* is derived from the French 'biais.'

II. i. 583. *Clapp'd on the outward eye.* 'Suddenly presented to the eye,—' (Moore-Smith). Possibly there is here another allusion to the game of bowls, since an aperture on one side of the bowl was called the eye.

II. i. 590. *fair angels.* Coins valued at ten shillings each. Used here as a pun. (Cf. III. iii. 8, 9; V. ii. 64.)

III. i. 59. *And made his majesty the bawd to theirs.* 'France has played a dishonorable part in uniting their other majesties, Fortune and King John, and France has been bribed by Fortune to play this part' (Moore-Smith).

III. i. 69-71. *For grief is proud and makes his owner stoop. To me and to the state of my great grief*

*Let kings assemble.* Grief makes the sufferer humble and thus itself is proud. Constance's grief is so proud that the two kings must come to her.

III. i. 78. *plays the alchemist.* Cf. Sonnet xxxiii:

'Full many a glorious morning have I seen . . .
Gilding pale streams with heavenly alchemy.'

III. i. 143. *Stephen Langton.* It was King John's wish that John Gray, Bishop of Norwich, be elected, in 1205, Archbishop of Canterbury. The Pope prevented this choice. Holinshed describes how the Pope 'procured by his papall authoritie the moonks of Canturburie . . . to choose one Stephan Langton . . . whom John refused to acknowledge.'

III. i. 147. *What earthy name to interrogatories.* 'What power on earth can force a king to answer questions put as to an accused person?'

III. i. 173. *excommunicate.* Pandulph's speech would suggest to the Elizabethan audience the excommunication of Queen Elizabeth by Pope Pius V, in 1570.

III. i. 207. *Forgo the easier.* 'To Blanch the curse of Rome seems the easier or lighter evil, because if Philip remains friendly with John, she will not be torn apart between her husband and her natural friends' (Moore-Smith).

III. i. 209. *new untrimmed bride.* In this much-discussed passage *new* probably means 'newly' and *untrimmed* 'divested' of bridal clothes. It is possible, however, that reference is made to the bride appearing at the altar with flowing hair, that is, with tresses untrimmed.

III. i. 211-216. *O! if thou grant my need, Which only lives but by the death of faith, That need must needs infer this principle, That faith would live again by death of need. O then, tread down my need, and faith mounts up; Keep my need up, and faith is trod-*

*den down!* 'O, if you will admit my need (distress), a need which exists merely because faith was not kept with me, that need is necessarily bound up with this principle, namely, that faith would once more live again, if my need were ended. O, then, if you will take away my need, faith will rise up, but if you continue my need, faith will still be trodden under foot.'

III. i. 233, 234. *And even before this truce, but new before, No longer than we well could wash our hands.* 'The interval between our hostility and our friendship was hardly enough time in which to wash our hands.'

III. i. 242. *Play fast and loose.* A gambling game, in which bets were made whether knots tied in a handkerchief or belt were fast or loose.

III. i. 259. *A cased lion.* Other readings are *chased, caged, chafed.* A cased lion is a lion angered by confinement.

III. i. 270-273. *For that which thou hast sworn to do amiss Is not amiss when it is truly done; And being not done, where doing tends to ill, The truth is then most done not doing it.* 'An act which you have sworn to commit unrighteously is not unrighteous if, after all, you perform it as truth requires; and in the case of an act which tends to evil, what truth requires is that it should not be performed at all' (Moore-Smith).

III. i. 275, 276. *though indirect, Yet indirection thereby grows direct.* 'Though giving up an evil course in this way is an indirect way of so doing, yet such an indirect method brings one back into the right course.'

III. i. 279-287. *It is religion that doth make vows kept, But thou hast sworn against religion: By what thou swear'st, against the thing thou swear'st, And mak'st an oath the surety for thy truth Against an oath; the truth thou art unsure To swear, swears only not to be forsworn; Else what a mockery should it be to swear! But thou dost swear only to be forsworn;*

*And most forsworn, to keep what thou dost swear.*
The Folio punctuation of the first two lines has been
restored.  Line 281 may then be taken as in apposi-
tion with these two lines.  A pause has been inserted
in line 283, after *oath.*  A paraphrase of the passage
follows: 'Religion is the cause of keeping vows, but
you have sworn against religion.  By so doing you
swear against the very thing by which you swear
(namely, religion), and you make this oath a warrant
of your truth as against the former oath.  This later
oath that you are so unreliable as to swear, is merely
a promise that you will not forswear yourself.  Without such a promise swearing would be a mockery.  But
you merely swear to forswear yourself, and so are
most certainly forsworn in adhering to your oath.'

III. i. 324.  *Old Time the clock-setter.*  Time is
compared to an old sexton, who regulates the clocks
and digs the graves.

III. ii. 2.  *airy devil.*  An allusion to the belief that
certain evil spirits live in the air.

III. ii. 5.  *Philip.*  Possibly an error.  Philip Faulconbridge's name had been changed to Sir Richard
Plantagenet (I. i. 161).

III. iii. 8, 9.  *imprison'd angels Set at liberty.*
Modern editors, following Sidney Walker, read *set at
liberty Imprison'd angels.*  (Cf. II. i. 590; V. ii. 64.)
The restoration of the Folio reading renders the metre
faulty.

III. iii. 12.  *Bell, book, and candle.*  Used with
reference to a form of excommunication which ended
with the words: 'Do to the book, quench the candle,
ring the bell!'

III. iii. 18.  *Come hither, little kinsman; hark, a
word.*  Elinor draws Arthur out of hearing, thus per-
mitting King John to broach his plan to Hubert.

III. iii. 39.  *Sound on into the drowsy race of night.*
Variant readings are: *one* for *on* and *ear* for *race.*

The Folio reading, *race,* may mean 'course' or 'passage.'

III. iv. 6, 7. *Are we not beaten? Is not Angiers lost? Arthur ta'en prisoner? divers dear friends slain?* These events occurred actually in different years. Arthur was captured and Elinor rescued at Mirabeau, in 1202. Angiers was conquered by King John in 1206.

III. iv. 44. *Thou art not [holy] to belie me so.* The reading of the Fourth Folio. The First Folio has *thou art holy,* a reading which can only be justified as ironical.

III. iv. 64. *wiry friends.* Rowe's correction of 'wiry fiends.'

III. iv. 68. *To England.* Constance alludes perhaps to King Philip's invitation, in line 20.

III. iv. 147, 148. *For he that steeps his safety in true blood Shall find but bloody safety and untrue.* 'He who to secure safety bathes himself in the blood of a true prince will find merely safety that is deceptive and that is productive of more bloodshed.'

III. iv. 167, 168. *And pick strong matter of revolt and wrath Out of the bloody fingers' ends of John.* 'And find good reasons for revolt in the crimes in which John has participated.'


IV. i. 2.. *arras.* The hangings of the room, of tapestry, named from Arras in Picardy.

IV. i. 98, 99. *Hubert, the utterance of a brace of tongues Must needs want pleading for a pair of eyes.* 'The words of two tongues would not be enough to plead for two eyes.'

IV. i. 122. *Well, see to live.* ' "Well, live, and live with the means of seeing," that is, "with your eyes uninjured" ' (Malone).

IV. ii. 91. *shears of destiny.* A reference to the myth of the Fates or Parcae. Atropos bore the shears and cut the thread of life.

**IV. ii. 119-123.** *My liege, her ear Is stopp'd with dust; the first of April died Your noble mother; and, as I hear, my lord, The Lady Constance in a frenzy died Three days before.* According to history Elinor died in July, 1204, and Constance on August 31, 1201.

**IV. ii. 211-214.** *And on the winking of authority To understand a law, to know the meaning Of dangerous majesty, when, perchance, it frowns More upon humour than advis'd respect.* 'When a person in authority winks, to interpret this as a command, to comprehend the meaning of a king in his darker moods, when, perhaps, he frowns more because of ill-temper than from deliberate consideration.'

**IV. iii. 4.** *ship-boy's semblance.* Arthur is disguised as a sailor-boy.

**IV. iii. 11.** *him.* Salisbury alludes to the Dauphin.

**IV. iii. 71.** *this hand.* Salisbury lifts up his hand as he pronounces his vow.

**IV. iii. 104.** *'Tis not an hour since I left him well.* Hubert apparently becomes aware now for the first time that Arthur is dead.

**V. i. 79.** *Our party may well meet a prouder foe.* 'Our army may meet successfully even a prouder foe than the French.'

**V. ii. 6.** *took the sacrament.* Solemnity was added to a covenant by having the parties to it take the eucharist together.

**V. ii. 36.** *gripple.* The First Folio has *cripple,* which is seemingly a printer's error. *Gripple* is Pope's correction.

**V. ii. 38.** *a vein of league.* A metaphor to describe the union of the two nations, forgetting their own quarrel for the new war. 'That is, make the angry blood of both flow, as it were, in one vein of alliance for crusading purposes' (Moberly).

**V. ii. 43, 44.** *O! what a noble combat hast [thou] fought Between compulsion and a brave respect!* In

the First, Second, and Third Folios the reading is
*hast fought*. Lewis refers to the conflict in Salisbury's
mind between the *compulsion* or necessity for acting
as he has acted, and the love he bears his own country.

V. ii. 64. *an angel spake.* Lewis thinks the appearance at this point of the pope's legate a divine
sanction of his words. Possibly there is also a play
on words connected with money: *purse* (line 61); *nobles* (line 62); and *angel* (line 64). An angel was the
fee for the opinion of a lawyer. (Cf. the play *Sir
Thomas More*, I. i. 176: 'there spake an angel.') (Cf.
also *King John*, II. i. 590; III. iii. 9.)

V. ii. 93. *I, by the honour of my marriage-bed.*
Lewis refers to his right to the lands by marriage,
through his wife, Blanch, the niece of King John.

V. ii. 144. *your nation's crow.* Probably an allusion to the gallic bird, the cock, with a derisive play
on the two meanings of *crow;* and also to the flight of
crows which dismayed the French at the battle of
Poitiers. See the play *Edward III*, IV. vi. 4, 5:

> 'The amazed French
> Are quite distract with gazing on the crows.'

V. iii. 8. *Swinstead.* An error, derived from the
old play, for Swineshead, in Lincolnshire.

V. iv. 24. *a form of wax.* An allusion to a tradition concerning witches: out of wax they made effigies
of living persons. By piercing or burning these figures they could injure in the same way the individuals
so represented. (Cf. Dante Gabriel Rossetti's ballad,
*Sister Helen.*)

V. vi. 12. *Unkind remembrance! thou and endless
night.* Hubert blames himself for his faulty memory.
This and the darkness have prevented recognition of
his friend. An emendation of the Folio *endless* is
*eyeless.*

**V. vii. 21, 22.**  *I am the cygnet to this pale faint swan, Who chants a doleful hymn to his own death.* An allusion to the well-known fable that the swan sang just before its death.  (Cf. *Othello*, V. ii. 245, 246: 'I will play the swan And die in music.')

**V. vii. 35.**  *ill fare.* Possibly a quibble on *fare* in the sense of food is intended.  Cf. *Hamlet* III. ii. 97-100.

**V. vii. 60.**  *heaven he knows.* The pronoun *he* refers to *heaven,* which has a personal sense, equivalent to 'God.'  Cf. III. i. 108: 'be husband to me, heavens.'

**V. vii. 74.**  *you stars.* Faulconbridge addresses the barons.

**V. vii. 110, 111.**  *O, let us pay the time but needful woe, Since it hath been beforehand with our griefs.* 'Let us indulge only in necessary mourning, since we have already paid in previous sorrows.'

# APPENDIX A

## Sources of the Play

*Kynge Johan,* an old play on the subject of King John's quarrels with the Pope, was written by John Bale, Bishop of Ossory, probably between 1557 and 1563. No evidence exists that Shakespeare knew of this play, or that it affected another play which was unquestionably his source. This drama appeared first anonymously in London in 1591, printed 'for Sampson Clarke.' It was in two parts, each bearing a separate title: *The Troublesome Raigne of Iohn King of England, with the discouerie of King Richard Cordelions Base sonne (vulgarly named, The Bastard Fawconbridge): also the death of King Iohn at Swinstead Abbey. As it was (sundry times) publikely acted by the Queenes Maiesties Players, in the honourable Citie of London;* and, *The Second Part of the troublesome Raigne of King Iohn, conteining the death of Arthur Plantaginet, the landing of Lewes, and the poysning of King Iohn at Swinstead Abbey. As it was (sundry times) publikely acted by the Queenes Maiesties Players, in the honourable Citie of London.* In 1611 the first and second parts were reprinted together. This edition bore the inscription 'Written by W. Sh.,' and the third edition in 1622 had Shakespeare's name in full: 'Written by W. Shakespeare,'—obvious attempts to capitalize on the commercial value of the dramatist's name.

The facts concerning the authorship of *The Troublesome Raigne* are unknown. Although the theory that Shakespeare wrote it has had, at various times, the support of the critics, Capell, Steevens, Tieck, Ulrici, there is no proof that this play was from his hand. Mr. Edward Rose in his *Shakespeare as an Adapter* even says: 'So entirely, indeed, has the dia-

logue been rewritten, that one can hardly imagine
Shakespeare to have known the original play except
by seeing it acted, and perhaps quickly reading it
through.'[1]  *The Troublesome Raigne,* produced in con-
fessed rivalry with Marlowe's *Tamburlaine,* was written about 1589, just after the repulse of the Spanish
armada.  Fleay found in it hints of the work of Greene,
Lodge, and Peele.  The best modern opinion favors
the authorship of the last-named poet.  A main source
was, of course, Holinshed's *Chronicles,* editions of
which appeared in 1577 and 1587, but many dates
and incidents in the old play are at variance with
history.[2]

A study of *The Troublesome Raigne* reveals its
creator's free use of history, and also its importance,
scene by scene, as source material for Shakespeare.
Although he constantly omitted and altered, *The Troublesome Raigne* and *King John* are so alike in theme
and general plan that even the dramatic weaknesses
of the older play persist in Shakespeare's version.  In
the former John inspires alternately our anger and
our sympathy.  He is domineering, murderous, and
weak, yet he is the representative of England against
papal tyranny.  In *King John* he arouses similar
feelings.  In the old play, too, are prefigurations of
Shakespeare's characters: the tender, lovable Arthur,
the queenly, despairing Constance, the manly, hu-

[1] *Macmillan's Magazine,* XXXIX, 69 ff., November, 1878.
[2] Some examples of the substantial independence of *The
Troublesome Raigne* from Holinshed are: the creation of
the character of Philip out of a very short passage in the
*Chronicles;* the story of Richard's slaying the lion; the iden-
tification of the Duke of Austria with the Viscount of
Limoges; the connection of the capture and recapture of
Angiers with the betrothal of Lewis and Blanch; the plunder
of the Abbeys by the Bastard; and the chronology respecting
Austria's death, the pilgrimage to Bury St. Edmunds, the
King's resignation of his crown, and the wreck on Goodwin
Sands.

morous, aggressive Bastard. *The Troublesome Raigne* is undistinguished by genius, but it must have seemed to Shakespeare, as it does now to us, potentially strong in characters and episodes of dramatic passion. Shakespeare uses only a few of the original lines; he cuts, emends, expands; but he bases his own tragedy on *The Troublesome Raigne.* There is indeed very little to suggest that he went behind this play for material, to Holinshed, Halle's *Chronicle,* or other sources.

Shakespeare's manipulation of the old play was characteristic. New dialogue, noble verse, different scenes, such as that between Hubert and Arthur, render King John a tragedy of character instead of a commonplace play on anti-Catholic issues. This ultra-Protestantism colors the whole of *The Troublesome Raigne,* obscuring character-portrayal. In this connection the following comments of Mr. Rose are suggestive concerning Shakespeare's use of *The Troublesome Raigne:* 'In reconstructing the play, the great want which struck Shakespeare seems to have been that of a strong central figure. He was attracted by the rough, powerful nature which he could see the Bastard's must have been; almost like a modern dramatist "writing up" a part for a star actor, he introduced Faulconbridge wherever it was possible, gave him the end of every act (except the third), and created, from a rude and inconsistent sketch, a character as strong, as complete, and as original as even he ever drew. Throughout a series of scenes, not otherwise very closely connected, this wonderfully real type of faulty, combative, not ignoble manhood is developed, a support and addition to the scenes in which he has least to say, a great power where he is prominent.

'This is the most striking example of his development of a character, but his treatment of Constance, Arthur, Hubert, Pandulph, and of some portions of the character of John himself, is very noticeable. The entire

wonderful scene in which Constance laments the loss of
her child is founded upon the seven lines:

"My tongue is tuned to story forth mishap:
 When did I breathe to tell a pleasing tale?
 Must Constance speak? Let tears prevent her talk.
 Must I discourse? Let Dido sigh, and say
 She weeps again to hear the wrack of Troy:
 Two words will serve, and then my tale is done—
 Eleanor's proud brat hath robbed me of my son!" [1]

Thus Shakespeare breathes into the confused collec-
tion of incidents new life. He makes Pandulph,
Salisbury, and Hubert human beings, and King John
a subtle and somewhat baffling character. Although
he actually omits four scenes and introduces no new
ones, the total effect is enrichment. Some of the minor
but significant changes are: at the time of the marriage contract between Lewis and Blanch, Constance
does not appear; most of the attacks on Rome are
excised, and notably the scene in which Faulconbridge
plunders the monasteries; the attitude of the Bastard
towards his illegitimacy becomes definitely ironical;
two long speeches of the Prophet, Peter of Pomfret,
disappear; the death of Arthur is treated with more
restraint, and the news of this is made concise and
dramatic; the poisoning of the King takes place off the
stage, and is unmotivated. A score of other alterations
might be noted, but such characteristic changes will
indicate Shakespeare's methods in wresting from *The
Troublesome Raigne* the elements for his own greater
clarity, subtlety, and emotional strength.

[1] Edward Rose (*op. cit.*), 71, 72.

# APPENDIX B

## The History of the Play

Francis Meres mentions Shakespeare's tragedy of *King John* in *Palladis Tamia* (1598). There is no record of a performance between 1598 and 1642, the date of the closing of the theatres. Yet it doubtless was produced at the 'Theatre' or 'Curtain' playhouse, Shoreditch, in or about 1596, when *Romeo and Juliet* was acted. If so, it is credible that Shakespeare acted in the tragedy, since he was one of the actual players in the Chamberlain's Company from 1594 to 1603. There is no evidence that *King John* was revived during the Restoration. Pepys does not mention it, nor does Dryden.

Colley Cibber's adaptation of the tragedy, *Papal Tyranny in the Reign of King John,* written about 1736, was never formally acted because of protests against thus meddling with Shakespeare.[1] Later, however, Cibber brought forward a version at Covent Garden, on February 15, 1745. Both these incidents caused productions of Shakespeare's *King John.* The first known performance of this was at Covent Garden Theatre on February 26, 1737. Of it Davies remarked: 'So much was said, and with propriety, by the critics who wrote against Cibber in the public prints, in commendation of Shakespeare's K. John, that Mr. Rich very wisely determined to take the hint, and resolved to revive the long-forgotten tragedy.

[1] 'Colley [Cibber] . . . went to the playhouse, and, without saying a word to any body, took the play from the prompter's desk, and marched off with it in his pocket. Pope, in his new edition of the Dunciad, . . . hints at the cautious conduct of the poet-laureat: "King John in silence modestly expires."' Thomas Davies, *Dramatic Miscellanies,* London, 1785, I, 5.

The principal parts, if I can trust my memory, were thus divided: King John, Mr. Delane; the Bastard, Tom Walker (the original Macheath); Hale acted the King of France, and Ryan Cardinal Pandulph; Lady Constance by Mrs. Hallam. . . . King John was acted several nights with great applause; but the king was not remarkably well represented by Delane; he could not easily assume the turbulent and gloomy passions of the character.'[1] Walker's Faulconbridge, however, was considered excellent, even superior to the later interpretations of the character by such actors as Garrick, Sheridan, Delane, and Barry. On February 2, 1738, the play was again acted, this time with a fresh prologue. Genest records further performances of *King John* on March 2 and November 29 of this year; and also on March 8, 1739, October 22, 1739, and April 2, 1741, all at Covent Garden.

Garrick first appeared in the title-rôle of *King John* at Drury Lane on February 20, 1745. Others in the cast were Delane as the Bastard, Barry as Hubert, Macklin as Pandulph, and Mrs. Cibber as Constance. Garrick in the following season in Dublin acted the parts of John and Faulconbridge, alternating in these with T. Sheridan. *King John* was not among Garrick's most successful plays, but records of a few remarkable interpretations have survived. Davies describes the scene (IV. ii.) between the King and Hubert: 'When Hubert shewed him his warrant for the death of Arthur, saying to him, at the same time,

Here is your hand and seal for what I did,

Garrick snatched the warrant from his hand; and, grasping it hard, in an agony of despair and horror, he threw his eyes to heaven, as if self-convicted of murder, and standing before the great Judge of the quick and dead to answer for the infringement of the

[1] Davies (*op. cit.*), I, 5-9.

divine command!'[1]  Mrs. Cibber's portrayal of Constance has been declared by some critics to have been greater than that of even Mrs. Siddons: 'When going off the stage, in this scene [III. iv.], she uttered the words,

O Lord! my boy!

with such an emphatical scream of agony, as will never be forgotten by those who heard her.'[2]  On March 2, 1745, this cast of the play gave its eighth performance.

On March 16, 1747, at Drury Lane *King John* was produced by Delane as a benefit performance.  It was again acted at Covent Garden on February 23, 1750, with Quin as the King, Barry as Faulconbridge, and Mrs. Cibber as Constance.  At a performance at the same theatre on April 25, 1751, the part of Constance was taken by Mrs. Woffington.  On January 23, 1754, *King John* was acted at Drury Lane with Garrick playing the Bastard, and Mossop the King.  In this rôle Garrick was unsuccessful.  'Various,' says Davies, 'have been the actors of this brave, generous, romantic, and humourous character, Faulconbridge: but, though Garrick, Sheridan, Delane, and Barry, have attempted it, they all fell short of the merits of Tom Walker. In him alone were the several requisites for the character: a strong and muscular person, a bold and intrepid look; manly deportment, vigorous action, and a humour which descended to an easy familiarity in conveying a jest or sarcasm with uncommon poignancy. Garrick had certainly much merit in the Bastard, but the want of the mechanical part was a deficiency not to be remedied by art.'[3]  It may be said that *King John* was now definitely restored to the English stage. Prior to Kemble's representation in 1783, Genest and

[1] Davies (*op. cit.*), I, 69, 70.
[2] *Ibid.*, I, 55, 56.
[3] *Ibid.*, I, 15.

other historians of the theatre record numerous performances. Some of the more notable were those beginning at Drury Lane, on December 17, 1760, with the elder Sheridan and Garrick exchanging the rôles of King John and Faulconbridge; that on February 2, 1774, with Mrs. Barry as Constance; and that on November 29, 1777, with Henderson as King John.

The next significant appearance of *King John* was at Drury Lane on December 10, 1783, with J. P. Kemble and Mrs. Siddons, 'Their majesties,' says Boaden, 'being desirous of seeing the brother and sister together.'[1] Kemble studied the part of the King under the guidance of the older Sheridan. This was one of several remarkable performances in which the chief rôles were taken by the Kemble family. Mrs. Siddons again played Constance and Kemble the King at Drury Lane on March 1, 1792, and May 13, 1801, and at Covent Garden on February 14, 1804. In the last-named performance Charles Kemble acted Faulconbridge. These interpretations of the King and of Constance made a deep impression upon stage tradition. Various critics, among them Hazlitt, thought Kemble's acting of King John painfully artificial, but Boaden says of the scene with Hubert: 'The most cold-blooded, hesitating, cowardly and creeping villany, that ever abused the gift of speech, found in Mr. Kemble the only powers competent to give it utterance. And if I were to select a scene, in the whole compass of the drama, more appropriate to him than any other, I should, I think, fix upon this noiseless horror, this muttered suggestion of slaughterous thought, on which the midnight bell alone was fitted to break, by one solitary undulating sound, that added to the gloom.'[2]

Likewise, Mrs. Siddons' rendering of the part, which

[1] James Boaden, *Memoirs of the Life of John Philip Kemble*, Philadelphia, 1825, p. 76.
[2] *Ibid.*, pp. 77, 78.

she herself called 'the majestic, the passionate, the tender,' evoked eloquent descriptions of her genius, especially in her pleas for vengeance and in her laments for Arthur.[1] One of the most memorable of these comments is her own, on her state of mind as she acted the part: 'Whenever I was called upon to personate the character of *Constance,* I never, from the beginning of the play to the end of my part in it, once suffered my dressing-room door to be closed, in order that my attention might be constantly fixed on those distressing events, which by this means, I could plainly hear going on upon the stage, the terrible effects of which progress were to be represented by me. Moreover, I never omitted to place myself, with *Arthur* in my hand, to hear the march, when, upon the reconciliation of England and France, they enter the gates of Angiers, to ratify the contract of marriage between the *Dauphin* and the *Lady Blanche:* because the sickening sounds of that march would usually cause the bitter tears of rage, disappointment, betrayed confidence, baffled ambition, and, above all, the agonizing feelings of maternal affection, to gush into my eyes. In short, the spirit of the whole drama took possession of my mind and frame, by my attention being incessantly riveted to the passing scene.'[2] We have also the testimony of Doran and Macready concerning the power of Charles Kemble's Faulconbridge.[3]

On December 3, 1816, Miss O'Neil appeared in *King John* as Constance. The Kembles continued to act in the tragedy during 1817, but the next distinctive performance was at Drury Lane on June 1, 1818. Edmund Kean played the King; Wallack, Faul-

[1] See James Boaden, *Memoirs of Mrs. Siddons,* Philadelphia, 1827, pp. 218-220.

[2] John William Cole, *The Life and Theatrical Times of Charles Kean,* London, 1859, II, 29.

[3] See John Doran, *Annals of the English Stage,* London, 1888, III, 213, and *Macready's Reminiscences* (ed. S. F. Pollock), New York, 1875, p. 401.

conbridge; and Miss Macauley, Constance.[1] On March
3, 1823, at Covent Garden Macready took the rôle of
John and Charles Kemble that of Faulconbridge.
Macready's *Diary* describes his success in this part,
which he repeated frequently before the close of 1842.

Two years later (1844) Samuel Phelps presented
the play at Sadler's Wells, acting during this season
the part of the King eighteen times. Marston was
Faulconbridge and Mrs. Warner, Constance. Phelps
and the younger Kean developed *King John* as a
spectacle. 'In the year 1846,' says Cole, 'Charles
Kean ventured on an experiment never before hazarded
in America—the production of the two historical
tragedies of "King John" and "Richard the Third,"
on a scale of splendour which no theatre in London
or Paris could have surpassed.'[2] Cole estimates
Charles Kean's interpretation of King John as inferior only to his Hamlet, Lear, Wolsey, and Shy-
lock. In this production Constance was played by
Miss Ellen Tree, and Arthur by Miss Kate Terry.
In the revival of 1858 Lacy acted Faulconbridge, Miss
Kate Terry, Blanch; Miss Ellen Terry (then ten years
old), Arthur, and Mr. Terry, King Philip.

Later English performances of *King John* have
been rare. Osmond Tearle produced it at Stratford-
on-Avon in February, 1890, and the Oxford Univer-

---

[1] See F. W. Hawkins, *The Life of Edmund Kean*, London,
1869, II, 50: 'His [Edmund Kean's] King John, without dis-
turbing the impression which John Kemble had created by
his performance of the character, was nobly represented.
The absolute triumph was won, as might be expected, in the
scene where he darkly intimated to Hubert his desire for
Arthur's death. Churchill's lines on Sheridan possessed the
full extent of their application here:

' "Behold him sound the depth of Hubert's soul,
    Whilst in his own contending passions roll;
    View the whole scene, with critic judgement scan,
    And then deny him merit if you can." '

[2] Cole (*op. cit.*), I, 343, 344.

sity Dramatic Society in February, 1891. The most
remarkable revival of these years was at the Hay-
market Theatre on September 20, 1899. The cast
included Mr. H. Beerbohm Tree as the King, Miss
Julia Neilson as Constance, and Mr. Lewis Waller as
Faulconbridge. The tragedy was compressed into
three acts, and, besides considerable new stage business, two tableaux were added: the battle before Angiers and the signing of the Magna Charta. *The
Saturday Review* of September 21 noted minor de-
fects but praised the dialogues between John and
Hubert. The Henry Talbot Dramatic Club acted the
tragedy at the Athenaeum, at Glasgow, in May, 1907.[1]
*King John* was presented again at Stratford in 1909,
1913, 1916, and once more in the spring of 1925. This
version was acted ten times. Altogether there were
nineteen performances of *King John* at Stratford between 1890 and 1925.[2]

*King John* was revived on Monday, September 4,
1926, at the Old Vic Theatre in London, with Duncan
Yarrow as the King, Baliol Holloway as the Bastard,
and Dorothy Massingham as Constance.[3]

Besides its vogue in England and America, *King
John* had success on the Continent. In Germany an
adaptation, *Arthur, Prinz von England,* was acted in
Altona, and published about 1801. In 1835 the Schle-
gel-Tieck version was presented at Düsseldorf. Stutt-
gart witnessed in 1850 an acting of Schlegel's version,
which in 1908 was performed at the Munich Hof-
Theater. Since the first production in America at the

[1] Portions of *King John* were acted by children of the
London County Council Schools at the Shakespeare Exhibi-
tion, at the Whitechapel Art Gallery, in the autumn of
1910. For references to these three last-mentioned performances of *King John,* see *Review of English Studies,* III, No.
10, April, 1927.

[2] See William Jaggard, *Shakespeare Memorial,* Stratford
[1926], pp. 11, 17, 19, 21, 26.

[3] See *The London Times,* September 6, 1926.

Southwark Theatre, Philadelphia, on December 12, 1768, with Douglass as the King, the play has been acted at regular intervals. Among these representations were performances at the John Street Theatre, New York, in 1769; at the Baltimore Theatre on December 10, 1782, with Heard as King John; at the Park Theatre, New York, on various dates between 1798 and 1832. Associated with the play were such actors as T. A. Cooper, G. F. Cooke, Macready, and the Kembles. *King John* was produced at the Bowery Theatre, New York, on April 30, 1834, with J. B. Booth as John, and at the Park Theatre on November 16, 1846, with Charles Kean as the King. Other actors connected with American productions from 1856 to 1909 were E. L. Davenport, J. McCullough, and Robert Mantell.[1]

The last American production of importance was Mantell's on March 8, 1909, at the New Amsterdam Theatre, New York. This *The Theatre* for April, 1909, though at variance with other criticisms, called 'a noble, impressive and adequate production.'[2]

[1] See G. O. Seilhamer, *History of the American Theatre*, Philadelphia, 1888, 1889, I, 242, 244, 249, 270, 317; II, 71, 77. On the American stage single scenes from *King John* were occasionally produced. See T. Allston Brown, *A History of the New York Stage*, New York, 1903, I, 15, 32, 36, 40, 42, 66, 124, 135, 212, 513; II, 429; III, 103. See also George C. D. Odell, *Annals of the New York Stage*, New York, 1927, I, 146; II, 176, 293, 317, 340, 366, 401, 477, 527, 555.

[2] See also *The Independent*, March 25, 1909; *The Literary Digest*, March 20, 1909; *The Nation*, March 11, 1909; *The New York Tribune*, March 9, 1909.

# APPENDIX C

The text of the present volume is, by permission of the Oxford University Press, that of the Oxford Shakespeare, edited by the late W. J. Craig. Craig's text has been carefully collated with the Shakespeare Folio of 1623, and the following deviations have been introduced:

1. The stage directions of the Folio have been restored. Speeches assigned by other editors to different characters have sometimes been ascribed again to the original speakers in the Folio, but in the case of two names for the same character, the modern name has ordinarily been retained (e.g. *Lewis* for *Dauphin*, *K. Phi.* for *France*). Necessary words and directions, omitted by the Folio, are added within square brackets.

2. Punctuation has been frequently altered, and spelling has been normalized to accord with modern English practice; e.g. Geoffrey, Poitiers, warlike, calfskin, villainy, fair play (instead of Geffrey, Poictiers, war-like, calf's-skin, villany, fair-play). The form 'and if,' where it occurs in the Folio, has been restored in place of 'an if.' So burthen, murther, etc., for burden, murder, murderer. The Folio has also been followed in the use of 'Cordelion' for 'Cœur-de-Lion,' and in the indication of slurred vowels, e.g. th' unsettled, th' advantage.

3. The following changes of text have been introduced, usually in accordance with Folio authority. The readings of the present edition precede the colon, while Craig's readings follow it.

I. i. 22   farthest F: furthest
   50   subject, I, a gentleman F: subject I, a gentleman
   134   Whether F: Whe'r

|         |                                                                                      |
|---------|--------------------------------------------------------------------------------------|
| 139     | Sir Robert's his F: Sir Robert his                                                   |
| 146     | I would F: I'd                                                                        |
| 152     | pound F: pounds                                                                       |
| 161     | rise F: arise                                                                         |
| 163     | th' mother's F: the mother's                                                          |
| 220     | 'tis F: it is                                                                         |
| II. i. 37 | to work our cannon F: to work: our cannon                                          |
| 106     | Geoffrey's in the name of God. F: Geffrey's, In the name of God                      |
| 119     | Excuse it is F: Excuse; it is                                                         |
| 144     | shoes F: shows                                                                        |
| 149     | King Lewis F: King,—Lewis                                                             |
| 177     | eldest F: eld'st                                                                      |
| 184     | he is F: he's                                                                         |
| 187, 188 | her plague; her sin his injury; Her injury the beadle to her sin: her plague, her sin; his injury Her injury, the beadle to her sin |
| 190     | And all for her, a plague upon her.  F: And all for her.  A plague upon her!          |
| 217     | doth F: do                                                                            |
| 234     | Craves F: Crave                                                                       |
| 250     | hath F: have                                                                          |
| 259     | rounder F: roundure                                                                   |
| 281     | you F: thou                                                                           |
| 289     | Sit's on's horseback F: Sits on his horse back                                       |
| 358     | equal potents, fiery kindled F: equal-potents, fiery-kindled                         |
| 371     | Kings of our fear F: Kings of ourselves                                              |
| 438     | as F: a                                                                               |
| III. i. 82 | holy day F: holiday                                                                |
| 147     | earthy F: earthly                                                                     |
| 259     | cased F: chafed                                                                       |
| 279, 280 | kept, But thou hast sworn against religion: F: kept; But thou hast sworn against religion |
| 294     | them.  But F: them; but                                                               |
| 320     | I will F: I'll                                                                        |
| iii. 8, 9 | imprison'd angels Set at liberty F: set at liberty Imprisoned angels                 |
| 26      | tune F: time                                                                          |
| 39      | on F: one                                                                             |
| 43      | heavy, thick F: heavy-thick                                                           |
| IV. i. 50 | lien F: lain                                                                        |
| 78      | heaven F: heaven's                                                                    |
| 92      | moth F: mote                                                                          |
| 122     | eye F: eyes                                                                           |

ii. 97  th' inheritance F: the inheritance
115  com s F: come
143  travail'd F: travell'd
216  accompt F: account
220  deeds ill done F: ill deeds done
iii. 41  You have F: Have you
155  center F: ceinture
**V. i.** 60  farther F: further
61  come F: comes
ii. 3  those F: these
10  zeal, and an F: zeal, an
27  stranger, march F: stranger march
41  wrastling F: wrestling
42  Doth F: Do
91  ye F: you
133  unheard F: unhair'd
v. 3  When English measure F: when the English
measur'd
**vi.** 12  endless F: eyeless
**vii.** 35  ill fare F: ill-fare
89  'tis F: it is

# APPENDIX D

## Suggestions for Collateral Reading

T. Davies: *Dramatic Miscellanies*. London, 1785, pp. 1-87.

W. Hazlitt: *Characters of Shakespear's Plays*. London, 1817.

Mrs. Anna Jameson: *Characteristics of Women*. London, 1833.

H. N. Hudson: *Shakespeare: His Life, Art, and Characters*. New York, 1848.

Edward Dowden: *Shakespeare: His Mind and Art*. London, 1875.

E. Rose: *Shakespeare as an Adapter* (Macmillan's Magazine). London, November, 1878.

George Brandes: *William Shakespeare, A Critical Study*. London, 1880.

F. S. Boas: *Shakespeare and His Predecessors*. New York, 1896.

G. C. Moore Smith (editor): *King John* (*Arden Shakespeare*). Boston, 1900. 'Introduction.'

S. A. Brooke: *Ten More Plays of Shakespeare*. London, 1913.

J. Munro and F. J. Furnivall: *Troublesome Raigne of King John* (*Shakespeare Classics*). London, 1913.

William Winter: *Shakespeare on the Stage* (Third Series). New York, 1916.

H. H. Furness, Jr.: *A New Variorum Edition of Shakespeare. The Life and Death of King John*. Philadelphia and London, 1919.

# INDEX OF WORDS GLOSSED

(Figures in full-faced type refer to page-numbers)

bend . . . solemn brows: **65** (IV. ii. 90)

bend: **25** (II. i. 379); **64** (IV. ii. 51)

bent (aimed): **12** (II. i. 37)

bent (inclined): **27** (II. i. 422)

bequeath: **6** (I. i. 149); **98** (V. vii. 104)

bestow yourself: **41** (III. i. 225)

blood (blood-relationship): **44** (III. i. 301)

blood (life): **65** (IV. ii. 99)

bloods (men of mettle): **21** (II. i. 278)

bloodshed: **74** (IV. iii. 55)

bloody: **70** (IV. ii. 210)

blots (blemishes): **35** (III. i. 45)

blots (calumniates): **16** (II. i. 132)

boisterous: **60** (IV. i. 95)

borne: **65** (IV. ii. 101)

borne, so evilly: **55** (III. iv. 149)

bosom: **56** (IV. i. 3)

bottoms: **14** (II. i. 73)

bounce: **28** (II. i. 462)

bound (enclose): **27** (II. i. 431)

bound (intending to go): **6** (I. i. 150)

bounden: **48** (III. iii. 29)

brabbler: **87** (V. ii. 162)

brac'd: **87** (V. ii. 169)

brav'd: **71** (IV. ii. 243)

brave: **87** (V. ii. 159)

bravely: **91** (V. v. 4)

brawl'd down: **25** (II. i. 383)

breach: **63** (IV. ii. 32)

break: **65** (IV. ii. 79)

break-vow: **32** (II. i. 569)

breath (life): **50** (III. iv. 19)

breath (utterance): **42** (III. i. 230)

breath, gap of: **51** (III. iv. 32)

breath'd (spoke): **63** (IV. ii. 36)

breathes (takes breath): **46** (III. ii. 4)

breathing (life): **90** (V. iv. 36)

beshrew: **90** (V. iv. 49)

brief: **93** (V. vi. 18)

brief in hand: **78** (IV. iii. 158)

brings . . . about: **36** (III. i. 81)

broke out: **93** (V. vi. 24)

broke with thee: **70** (IV. ii. 227)

broker: **32** (II. i. 568)

brooded: **49** (III. iii. 52)

buss: **51** (III. iv. 35)

but (except): **36** (III. i. 92)

but (if . . . not): **13** (II. i. 43); **90** (V. iv. 50)

but (merely): **59** (IV. i. 66)

but (that . . . not): **61** (IV. i. 128)

but for because: **33** (II. i. 588)

buy out: **39** (III. i. 164)

call: **56** (III. iv. 174)

canker (like a canker worm): **53** (III. iv. 82)

canker (ulcer): **82** (V. ii. 14)

canker'd (malignant): **18** (II. i. 194)

canonized: **39** (III. i. 177)

capable of: **29** (II. i. 476)

carriages: **97** (V. vii. 90)

cast away: **92** (V. v. 13)

censured: **23** (II. i. 328)

center: **78** (IV. iii. 155)

chaps: **24** (II. i. 352)

charge (noun): **65** (IV. ii. 75)

charge (verb): **39** (III. i. 151)

charity: **56** (III. iv. 173)

check: **16** (II. i. 123)

choice: **14** (II. i. 72)

christendom: **57** (IV. i. 16)

churlish: **30** (II. i. 519)

circle (circuit): **86** (V. ii. 136)

circle (crown): **78** (V. i. 2)

circumstance: **14** (II. i. 77)

civil tumult: **71** (IV. ii. 247)

clap . . . up: **42** (III. i. 235)

clearly: **91** (V. v. 7)

climate: **24** (II. i. 344)

clippeth: **82** (V. ii. 34)

close aspect: **64** (IV. ii. 72)

closely: **62** (IV. i. 133)

closet: **72** (IV. ii. 267)

clouts, babe of: **52** (III. iv. 58)

cocker'd silken wanton: **81** (V. i. 70)

coil: **17** (II. i. 165)

coldly: **13** (II. i. 53); **88** (V. iii. 13)

commend: **83** (V. ii. 56)

comment: **72** (IV. ii. 263)

commodity, tickling: **32** (II. i. 573)

companies: **68** (IV. ii. 167)

complete of: **27** (II. i. 434)

composition (agreement): **32** (II. i. 561)

composition (constitution): **4** (I. i. 88)

compound: **21** (II. i. 281)

conceit: **48** (III. iii. 50)

concludes: **5** (I. i. 127)

condition: **46** (III. i. 341)

conduct (escort): **2** (I. i. 29)

conduct (leadership): **67** (IV. ii. 129)

confine: **71** (IV. ii. 246)

confound: **63** (IV. ii. 29)

confound themselves: **95** (V. vii. 20)

confounded: **96** (V. vii. 58)

confusion: **24** (II. i. 359)

conjure: **72** (IV. ii. 269)

conscience, no: **70** (IV. ii. 229)

consequently: **71** (IV. ii. 240)

consideration: **63** (IV. ii. 25)

contagious: **90** (V. iv. 33)

contemn'd: **82** (V. ii. 13)

content: **35** (III. i. 42)

contrary: **69** (IV. ii. 198)

controlment: **2** (I. i. 20)

conversion, for your: **8** (I. i. 189)

convertite: **79** (V. i. 19)

convicted: **50** (III. iv. 2)

coops: **12** (II. i. 25)

copy: **66** (IV. ii. 113)

correct: **14** (II. i. 87)

corrupted: **39** (III. i. 166)

corruptibly: **94** (V. vii. 2)

countercheck: **19** (II. i. 224)

counterfeit: **37** (III. i. 99)

counties: **79** (V. i. 8)

cousin: **45** (III. i. 339)

cracker: **16** (II. i. 147)

crafty: **59** (IV. i. 53)

create: **61** (IV. i. 107)

cries out upon: **82** (V. ii. 19)

cry aim: **18** (II. i. 196)

cunning: **59** (IV. i. 54)

customed: **55** (III. iv. 155)

darkly: **70** (IV. ii. 232)

date: **76** (IV. iii. 106)

day: **54** (III. iv. 116)

dead news: **97** (V. vii. 65)

deal: **82** (V. ii. 22)

dear (grievous): **10** (I. i. 257)

dear (heartfelt): **17** (II. i. 157)

death, took it on his: **5** (I. i. 110)

deceit: **9** (I. i. 215)

deep-sworn: **42** (III. i. 231)

defy: **51** (III. iv. 23)

denounce: **45** (III. i. 319)

deny their office: **61** (IV. i. 119)

departed: **32** (II. i. 563)

device: **8** (I. i. 210)

dew: **83** (V. ii. 45)

difference: **42** (III. i. 238)

diffidence: **3** (I. i. 65)

dim: **53** (III. iv. 85)

disallow of: **1** (I. i. 16)

discipline: **12** (II. i. 39); **26** (II. i. 413)

discontents: **78** (IV. iii. 151)

dishabited: **19** (II. i. 220)

dispatch: **57** (IV. i. 27)

dispiteous: **58** (IV. i. 34)

dispos'd (regulated): **50** (III. iv. 11)

dispose: **10** (I. i. 263)

disposing: **98** (V. vii. 92)

distemper'd: **73** (IV. iii. 21)

distemper'd day: **55** (III. iv. 154)

dogged: **78** (IV. iii. 149)

doom: **44** (III. i. 311)

doth: **19** (II. i. 217)

doubt: **57** (IV. i. 19)

doubtful: **80** (V. i. 36)

doubtless: **61** (IV. i. 130)

draw: **45** (III. i. 339)

draws: **17** (II. i. 169)

drawn: **66** (IV. ii. 118)

drift: **26** (II. i. 412)

dubb'd: **10** (I. i. 245)

dust: **54** (III. iv. 128)

easy: **2** (I. i. 36)

effect: **58** (IV. i. 38)

else (if it is not believed): **61** (IV. i. 108)

else (other kinds): **21** (II. i. 276)

embassy: **1** (I. i. 6)

embattailed: **69** (IV. ii. 200)

embounded: **77** (IV. iii. 137)

embrace: **73** (IV. iii. 12)

endamagement: **19** (II. i. 209)

endless: **93** (V. vi. 12)

enflam'd: **78** (V. i. 7)

enforce: **28** (II. i. 448)

enforced: **82** (V. ii. 30)

enfranchisement: **64** (IV. ii. 52)

English: **91** (V. v. 3)

entertain: **54** (III. iv. 133)

envenom: **35** (III. i. 63)

envy: **52** (III. iv. 73)

error: **19** (II. i. 230)

estate: **66** (IV. ii. 128)

evilly borne, so: **55** (III. iv. 149)

example: **50** (III. iv. 13)

exampled: **74** (IV. iii. 56)

exclamation: **32** (II. i. 558)

exercise: **64** (IV. ii. 60)

exhalation: **55** (III. iv. 153)

expectation: **62** (IV. ii. 7)

expedient (expeditious): **13** (II. i. 60); **19** (II. i. 223); **72** (IV. ii. 268)

expedition: **14** (II. i. 79)

extends: **61** (IV. i. 120)

extremes: **61** (IV. i. 108); **95** (V. vii. 13)

eye, unthread the rude: **89** (V. iv. 11)

eye of heaven: **62** (IV. ii. 15)

faint: **91** (V. v. 4)

faintly: **70** (IV. ii. 227)

fair-play orders: **81** (V. i. 67)

fair writ: **58** (IV. i. 37)

faithless: **19** (II. i. 230)

faiths, mended: **97** (V. vii. 75)

fall: **4** (I. i. 78)

fall from: **45** (III. i. 320)

fall over: **38** (III. i. 127)

fall'n off, are . . .: **92** (V. v. 11)

fantasied: **67** (IV. ii. 144)

fantasies: **95** (V. vii. 18)

fare, ill: **95** (V. vii. 35)

fault: **63** (IV. ii. 33)

favour (appearance): **90** (V. iv. 50)

favour (permission): **27** (II. i. 422)

fearful: **66** (IV. ii. 106)

fearfully believe: **64** (IV. ii. 74)

fear not you: **57** (IV. i. 7)

feature: **16** (II. i. 126); **72** (IV. ii. 264)

fell: **94** (V. vii. 9)

fell anatomy: **51** (III. iv. 40)

fellowship: **50** (III. iv. 3)

fence: **22** (II. i. 290)

festival: **36** (III. i. 76)

fetch about: **63** (IV. ii. 24)

figur'd: **83** (V. ii. 53)

figure: **90** (V. iv. 25)

fine: **90** (V. iv. 38)

fitting to: **93** (V. vi. 19)

flat: **44** (III. i. 298)

flatly: **86** (V. ii. 126)

fleet: **21** (II. i. 285)

flesh: **81** (V. i. 71)

fleshly: **71** (IV. ii. 245)

flood (flowing in of the tide): **97** (V. vii. 64)

flood (sea): **50** (III. iv. 1)

fond: **53** (III. iv. 92)

fondly: **20** (II. i. 258)

foot, on: **56** (III. iv. 169)

footing: **81** (V. i. 66)

for: **33** (II. i. 591)

for that: **90** (V. iv. 42)

forage: **80** (V. i. 59)

force perforce: **38** (III. i. 142)

forced: **65** (IV. ii. 98)

'fore: **78** (V. i. 7)

forethought: **44** (III. i. 312)

form (image): **71** (IV. ii. 256)

form (orderly arrangement): **42** (III. i. 253); **53** (III. iv. 101)

form (outward aspect): **90** (V. iv. 50)

form (portrait): **95** (V. vii. 32)

forth: **67** (IV. ii. 148)

forwearied: **20** (II. i. 233)

from: **60** (IV. i. 86)

from all indifferently: **32** (II. i. 579)

from forth: **90** (V. iv. 45)

fronts: **24** (II. i. 356)

full: **83** (V. ii. 59)

fulsome: **51** (III. iv. 32)

gall: **76** (IV. iii. 94)

gap of breath: **51** (III. iv. 32)

garnish: **62** (IV. ii. 15)

gawds: **48** (III. iii. 36)

general: **73** (IV. iii. 17)

gentle: **68** (IV. ii. 159)

get: **10** (I. i. 259)

gilt: **23** (II. i. 316)

give off: **79** (V. i. 27)

give us leave: **9** (I. i. 230)

God-a-mercy: **8** (I. i. 185)

golden hand, with her: **35** (III. i. 57)

good den: **8** (I. i. 185)

good world: **76** (IV. iii. 116)

goods: **64** (IV. ii. 64)

go to: **60** (IV. i. 97)

got: **5** (I. i. 108)